DANCING WITH DINOSAURS

To Friday,
twentieth day of April, 1951,
first footprints in the sand
towards discoveries in this book,
sixty years later: 20/04/2011.

Mark Patrick Hederman

Dancing with Dinosaurs
A Spirituality for the 21st Century

the columba press

First published in 2011 by
ᴄhe ᴄolumʙᴀ pʀess
55A Spruce Avenue, Stillorgan Industrial Park,
Blackrock, Co Dublin

Cover by Emmaus O'Herlihy OSB
Origination by The Columba Press
Printed in Ireland by Brunswick Press Ltd, Dublin

ISBN 978 1 85607 735 4

Acknowledgements
Biblical quotations are from the NRSV. Audre Lorde, 'Father, Son and
Holy Ghost' from *Collected Poems of Audre Lorde*. Copyright © 1997 by
The Audre Lorde Estate. Reprinted with the permission of W. W.
Norton & Company, Inc.

Contents

Introduction

My task is to clarify the landscape between this world and the next. Others have the job of explaining everything else that exists; mine is simple and straightforward: how do we relate to God? And in this I am helped, not just by the many people who surround me, but also by the Holy Spirit who continually prompts and guides. This is the tenth book I have written since we turned the corner into the new millennium. Each book seeks to clarify another aspect of this great relationship. Information comes from sources too many to be numbered but each one derives from direct intervention of the Spirit. Of the billion facts available at every moment, why should this particular one find itself on my radar screen? Because it has been put there by an ever-patient amanuensis anxious to have the Trinity translated into words. Sometimes I do not understand what is being suggested to me. I simply record it and, in time, the significance dawns. Waking up early one morning the mystery clicks into shape. Because I am a slow learner, I repeat myself from book to book. The reality I am pointing towards is always the same, even if it is now being approached from a different angle. Repetition clarifies in a new context. Progress is gradational and incremental.

In the beginning I get obsessed with a certain theme. Gregory Collins, with whom I share a theological passion, much more scholarly and articulate in him, suggests that this book is my way of dealing with the fact that, nearly three years ago now, I agreed to become officially part of the establishment of the Roman Catholic Church by being ordained to the priesthood on 8 December 2008.

Be that as it may, I knew the theme I was being pushed to develop when Justin Sammon invited me to address a Turas na mBan Conference in Westport on Saturday 13 October 2007. The *Examiner* newspaper carried a coloured supplement on dinosaurs some days before which pressed a buzzer in my brain. What happens after this initial seed is sown is that I am invited to give various talks in different places which I use to develop my theme and these make up the chapters of the eventual book. So the book gets written by an agency other than myself, which I believe to be the Holy Spirit, who also arranges the different invitations and sometimes prompts the organisers of the talks to push me in a particular direction. The following, therefore, represents some of the itinerary which accompanied the writing of this book.

Saturday 7 October 2007, Prince Albert II of Monaco awarded the second Princess Grace Humanitarian prize to Sacha, Duchess of Abercorn, during the Ireland fund of Monaco Gala dinner at the Hotel Hermitage. Sacha invited me to Monaco for the occasion. Colum McCann was the chosen author addressing a lunch party in Roquebrune, the last dwelling place on earth of W. B. Yeats, the afternoon before the ceremony. He had received The Ireland Fund of Monaco Literary Award in Memory of Princess Grace five years before in 2002. This prize had been created to commemorate the twentieth anniversary of the death of Princess Grace in September 1982. Two years after we met, Colum McCann's novel *Let the Great World Spin* (2009) appeared and my sister Louise insisted that it be read. So, I was ready for it.

Chuck and Helga Feeney invited me to the second annual University of Limerick Chancellor's Concert on 24 March 2010. I was sitting beside Roger Downer, former president of the university. He told me about research being done in Limerick concerning ourselves as undeveloped foetuses and the implications of this for our brains. Roger was working with Dr Stuart Shanker, whom I googled on the Internet, and this led me to the work of Dr Paul MacLean. Later as I was working on the chapter about our triune brain, Senan Furlong gave me the book he was reading, *A General Theory of Love*, by Thomas Lewis MD, Fari Amini MD, and Richard Lannon MD, which provided precisely the piece of the jig-saw I was missing.

Then the pace hotted up. Caroline Cunningham asked me to give a talk to the lawyers of GECAS in Dromoland Castle on 8 June 2010.

Saturday 31 July 2010, John Hill and I drove to Dublin after he had given our community retreat. I returned by train next day which was a Sunday. The shop in the Irish Film Centre was open, as I walked by towards the train, and the film *Man on Wire* fell off the shelf. We used it the following week for the summer course on 'Icons, Chant, Cinema and Symbolism.' It was a high risk dance with the dinosaurs.

A month later Pfizer's in Ringaskiddy asked me to give an 'inspirational' talk to their assembled staff on what they called a 'chill pill day' of 10 August 2010.

I was invited by Michael Screene to Croí Nua Spirituality Centre in Galway on 10 November 2010, and to the Ursuline Convent in Blackrock, Cork on Sunday 6 January 2011, where I developed the chapters on The Church as Dinosaur and the Second Vatican Council. The Limerick/Thomond Probus Society invited me to speak on the day after St Valentine's Day, 15 February 2011, where I gave them an introduction to the dinosaur behind the rose bush.

Cleo Webster recommended the book by A. Jean Ayers, *Sensory Integration and the Child*, while I was staying with Elizabeth Shannon, as always, in 25 Lenox Street, Brookline, Massachusetts.

Fanny Howe read the first draft of my manuscript with helpful disbelief and then, with her usual intuitive aplomb, carved the dinosaur into edible parts (not chapters). Martin Browne proofread with characteristic indefectibility. Emmaus O'Herlihy designed the cover with nimble choreography and Seán O Boyle put the pieces together. To these, and to the patient Glenstal community whose forbearance borders, at times, on insouciance, my grateful thanks.

I cannot end a book on dinosaurs without a last special mention of the oldest member of our community, Dom Placid Murray, who celebrates this year his 70th anniversary of ordination to the priesthood. He will certainly take no responsibility for what I say here about John Henry Newman, to whose works he has devoted a lifetime of scholarship. May they both be blessed.

PART ONE

Dinosaurs in general

Genesis 3: The Fall

Now the serpent was more crafty than any of the wild animals the LORD God had made. He said to the woman, "Did God really say, 'You must not eat from any tree in the garden'?" The woman said to the serpent, "We may eat fruit from the trees in the garden, but God did say, 'You must not eat fruit from the tree that is in the middle of the garden, and you must not touch it, or you will die.'" "You will not certainly die," the serpent said to the woman. "For God knows that when you eat from it your eyes will be opened, and you will be like God, knowing good and evil."

When the woman saw that the fruit of the tree was good for food and pleasing to the eye, and also desirable for gaining wisdom, she took some and ate it. She also gave some to her husband, who was with her, and he ate it. Then the eyes of both of them were opened, and they realised they were naked; so they sewed fig leaves together and made coverings for themselves.

Then the man and his wife heard the sound of the LORD God as he was walking in the garden in the cool of the day, and they hid from the LORD God among the trees of the garden. But the LORD God called to the man, "Where are you?" He answered, "I heard you in the garden, and I was afraid because I was naked; so I hid." And he said, "Who told you that you were naked? Have you eaten from the tree that I commanded you not to eat from?" The man said, "The woman you put here with me – she gave me some fruit from the tree, and I ate it."

Then the LORD God said to the woman, "What is this you have done?" The woman said, "The serpent deceived me, and I ate."

So the LORD God said to the serpent, "Because you have done this, cursed are you above all livestock and all wild animals! You will crawl on your belly and you will eat dust all the days of your life. And I will put enmity between you and the woman, and between your offspring and hers; he will crush your head, and you will strike his heel."

This is an inspired mythical way of describing the combat which human nature will always wage between the horizontal and the vertical in its make up.

Dinosaurs have been described as the most successful animals that ever inhabited this planet. They were the dominant terrestrial vertebrates for over 160 million years, from the late Triassic period (about 230 million years ago) until the end of the Cretaceous period (about sixty-five million years ago). We had to learn how to live with them, and survive in spite of them. Not only that, in the evolution of life on the planet we have a common ancestry. Somewhere along the line a dinosaur leaped over the wall. We are descended from a smaller more compact version of these outsized monsters and this littleness must have helped us to live through the Cretaceous-Tertiary extinction event which obliterated the rest of them. However, there is an undeniably reptilian streak in our make-up. On the other hand, or claw if you prefer, if the dinosaurs had not been mysteriously wiped out in some catastrophic happening sixty-five million years ago, they might still be around today – and we might not.

No one can say exactly what happened to eliminate them, and there are many theories pieced together from remaining evidence on this side of the divide. All we have to go on are fragmented remains buried after the crash from which many ingenious and hardworking experts have pieced together a picture of what might have been before.

A meteorite strike seems to be the most likely explanation. Part of an asteroid some ten kilometres wide must have slammed into the earth where we now situate Mexico's Yucatan peninsula. Millions of creatures were killed by the impact of the strike which in seconds blasted out a crater 175 kilometres wide. The impact threw up tonnes of rock and dust into the atmosphere, triggering earthquakes, volcanoes and tsunamis on land and sea, blocking out the sun and making darkness spread over the earth. Temperatures sank and the few remaining dinosaurs to survive the initial impact must have died of starvation or exposure.

We, as a human species, are comparatively recent arrivals on earth in the form and shape we now enjoy. Since the disappearance of our giant brothers and sisters we belong to a biological species which is, for better or for worse, definitively in charge of the planet. However, in the strange history of life on our planet we are descended from the dinosaurs:

> Early mammals evolved from small, lizardfish reptiles. The peculiar mammalian innovation – carrying developing young within a warm-blooded body rather than leaving them outside in eggs – had been established well before an errant asteroid rammed the planet and put the chill on the dinosaurs. The rapid demise of the reptilian giants left open opportunities for an upwardly mobile class. Mammals scurried into the gap and bred like the rabbits they were to become. Sixty-five million years later, the Age of Mammals is still in full swing.[1]

Homo Sapiens, as we have been taught to label our particular blend of mammal, has been on earth perhaps 50,000 years. Those of us who have seen films such as *Jurassic Park* will be aware of what it was like to live in a world where other species were in charge and where we were like irrelevant insects crushed between claw and hoof. It took us, with a great deal of evolutionary effort, several thousand years to produce the first billion of our species; now, in this blessed twenty-first century, we are producing a billion every ten to fifteen years. We have subjugated the other species. We are not just in charge, but we're here to stay. Unless, of course, we wipe ourselves out as happened to the dinosaurs.

Once the dinosaurs had disappeared, it took thousands of years before those of us remaining on the planet were able to piece together the evidence and work out what had happened and what they must have looked like. People have been finding dinosaur fossils for thousands of years, but it never occurred to any of us what their provenance might be. There are references to 'dragon' bones found in China, by an author called Chang Qu, over 2,000 years ago. The Greeks and the Romans identified ogres or griffins from oversize fossil remains which puzzled

---

1. *A General Theory of Love*, Thomas Lewis MD, Fari Amini MD, Richard Lannon MD, Vintage Books, New York, 2000, p 24

them. In 1676, a huge thigh bone was found in England and was thought to be the remains of a giant. In fact it was part of a large, meat-eating dinosaur that lived about 180 million years before. But no one on earth even imagined that such a creature could have existed until William Buckland, a British clergyman and amateur palaeontologist, described it scientifically in 1824 and called it *Megalosaurus*, which meant 'great lizard'. *Megalosaurus Bucklandii* as it was named after himself, was the first dinosaur to be scientifically classified. Then the penny began to drop and our imaginations combined with our discoveries to allow the unthinkable to be thought.

The first nearly-complete dinosaur skeleton was discovered in 1838, and soon we began to imagine what a world populated by such creatures might have been like. The term 'dinosaur' was coined in 1842 by the English palaeontologist Richard Owen, from the Greek δεινός (*deinos*) meaning 'terrible, powerful,' and σαῦρος (*sauros*) meaning 'lizard'. It is only, therefore, within the last two hundred years that we have come to know anything about dinosaurs, and only in the last fifty that we have gone dinosaur mad. Throughout the first half of the twentieth century, most scientists mistakenly believed that dinosaurs were sluggish, unintelligent cold-blooded animals. However, research since the 1970s has indicated that they were highly active and well adapted for social intercourse. So, we're dealing with highly intelligent and manipulative monsters!

In case you haven't noticed, we have bred our own species of dinosaur. And in this second decade of the twenty-first century, unless we become fully aware of this and learn how to dance with these dinosaurs, we too could be crushed between their extremities.

Where are they? Who are they? Dinosaurs as a species are diverse and varied, but, without putting a tooth in it, as they say, you are probably working for one; you may be investing your money in one; and, if you are a believer, you are likely to be worshipping in one. Churches, banks and multinationals are some of the modern breed of dinosaur.

Perhaps it might be true to say that unless a pioneering brainwave turns into a lumbering dinosaur it has little hope of surviving the vicissitudes of history. So many religions, political parties and businesses have thrived for a few inspiring and energetic years before collapsing into oblivion. Statistics supplied by sociologists (mostly in America) suggest that 75% of small businesses fail in their first five years and 50% of the remainder collapse by their tenth year. Small may be beautiful, but in the world in which we live it is not very durable.

The rapid rise of multinational corporations, the more recent breed of dinosaur, has been of concern to many who see them as a threat to human and civil rights. Naysayers point out that such multinationals create false needs in consumers and have a long history of interference in local politics. They often donate massive corporate campaign contributions to political parties, ensuring that their friends remain in power. Such negative arguments are illustrated and supported every day by global news stories about corporate corruption. However, all such complaints are futile if their intention is to try to rid us of the species. The dinosaurs are here to stay, and only the most robust will survive. There is no point in moaning about their existence or suggesting that you are not prepared to play the game of life until they are all removed from the playing pitch. They will be here long after your protest has ended. Those of us who plan to continue, have to learn how to dance with the dinosaurs rather than allow them to crush us.

European history attaches particular significance to the shift from the feudal institutions of the Middle Ages to the modern varieties of dinosaur which characterise contemporary life. During the period of the industrial revolution in Europe, as an example, many countries went through a period of 'institutionalisation', which saw governments themselves turning into dinosaurs, monolithic juggernauts driving into areas seen previously as essentially the private sphere. But what about those dinosaurs we have to contend with who have survived even beyond the Middle Ages and whose history stretches back over thousands of years?

The more recent phenomenon of 'globalisation' gives the dinosaur the whole planet as a playground. The MNC breed (multinational corporations) disport themselves in more than one country. 'Corporate giants' have been sighted as early as 1897, developing a distinctive dynamic of 'expand or expire'.

Some have budgets exceeding the GDPs of small countries. These influence the way the world goes round. Regional economies are absorbed into the globalised economy in an ever-expanding network. Countries compete to court the MNC dinosaur, which brings increases in employment, economic activity, and tax revenue. Courting means offering incentives: tax breaks, government assistance, improved infrastructures; ethically, it means a race to the bottom, discarding whatever might alienate the beast in terms of environmental standards or labour requirements.

Most of us imagine that such institutions are part of the natural, unchanging landscape of human history. They are not. These dinosaurs are constructs of a particular time, culture and society. They are produced by us. But although they are made by us they are still unavoidable. Something in our nature, which comes from the dinosaur, impels us to construct mirror images of our terrifying ancestors as external correlatives of ourselves. It is as if, inside every tiny human being, there is a dinosaur trying to get out. Unless your business is big and boisterous, it is never going to endure.

* * *

Less than five hundred years ago, we came across the first dinosaurs of the MNC variety. What coaxed them out of hiding was gluttonous attraction towards spices. Joseph, in the Hebrew Bible, was sold into slavery by his brothers to spice merchants. So also, rivalry between nations for control of the spice trade led to capture and betrayal on the grand scale. The Dutch East India Company can be identified as the first multinational mega corporation. It wielded quasi-governmental power, waging wars, negotiating treaties, coining money, and establishing colonies. Its British counterpart, founded by Royal Charter signed by Queen Elizabeth I, on 31 December 1600, became 'The Company of Merchants of London trading into the East Indies.' Setting off for the Banda Islands to trade woollen cloth and silver for the coveted spices, they found that the Dutch had got there before them. *Verenigde Oostindische Compagnie* (VOC), the Dutch East India Company, had been granted by their own government a monopoly on all trade in the East Indies. During its 200 year history the VOC became the largest dinosaur of its kind.

In 1623, on the clove island of Amboina, the battle of the dinosaurs took place. The Dutch were victorious. They tortured and executed English and Japanese traders. The English East India Company then concentrated on trade with India itself, establishing a base in Madras. By this time in England tea had become a national addiction. In the late 1700s it accounted for more than 60% of the East India Company's total trade. 'Here thou, great Anna, whom three realms obey/doth sometimes council take, and sometimes tea,' Alexander Pope in 1712 described Hampton Court, the royal palace where Queen Anne, last monarch of the House of Stuart, presided. Tea and spices were all the rage but what could they trade for such delights? The English became concerned that too much of the family silver was leaving their shores. They changed their barter for addictive opium, leaving in their wake a widespread drug problem especially in China.

In 1753, the wealthy Mughal Empire weakened, and wars broke out between different districts of India. Robert Clive, a member of the British East India Company, recaptured Calcutta at the Battle of Plassey. So it was that the English dinosaur became responsible for the whole of Bengal, India's richest province. Land taxes tripled and many Indians were reduced to poverty. Millions died in famine, and over the next two decades, so many more were dispossessed of their land. By 1773 even the British government became concerned about the ravages of their own dinosaur in these Indian territories. They decided to curb its power. Exclusive trade with India was stopped even though trade with China continued. This dinosaur was finally destroyed in 1858 after a rebellion by its Bengali Army.

* * *

Every year the world provides images both for the dinosaur and how to dance with it. 2010 was the year when the whole world held its breath as we watched thirty-three Chilean miners being released from entrapment from the copper mines at San José.

Never before have so many been trapped underground for so long. Beginning at midnight on Tuesday, 12 October 2010, the rescue operation exceeded expectations at every step. Officials first said it might be four months before they could get the men out; it turned out to be sixty-nine days and eight hours. Such human ingenuity and the triumph of engineering, mirrors the way in which we can dance with the dinosaur and escape entrapment. However, even though we all enjoyed the understandable elation, first of all of finding the men alive and then watching their protracted rescue, we cannot lose sight of the dinosaur which caused the disaster in the first place.

Chile is the world's leading producer of copper. The price of copper at a record high was driving companies to extract as much ore as possible while the boom lasted. Mining was getting more dangerous all over Chile. The owners of the San José mine had failed to install alternate exit routes, as required by law. When the miners first made contact with the outside world, eighteen days after the initial explosion, they had to be told that the legally mandated emergency ladder didn't exist. The evacuation exit remained clear for forty-eight hours and they could have escaped during that two-day period, if the ladder had been there.

The government had, apparently, ordered the mine to be shut down for safety reasons in 2006 and 2007. When the owners heard of the disaster they were on the brink of bankruptcy and could not afford to pay the miners' wages while they were trapped underground.

The San Esteban mining company therefore turned over the rescue operation to a state owned company since they had no money to pay for it. So, the real question is how a mining company so deep in debt and with so little income was able to maintain its operations for so long. And the answer must be: by cutting corners and risking the lives of their workforce. It is only when the global spotlight is focused on this troubled mine, these buried miners, that such basic problems become visible. One wonders what would happen if this spotlight were turned on the great underground dinosaur which is the total mining industry of Chile?

* * *

Even a rose by any other name can become a dinosaur plant. Every time 14 February comes around most of us buy at least one red rose for the person we love. This is because it is the feast of St Valentine. Who is St Valentine? And why would we give roses to each other on his feast day? What matter the reasons?

Surely this must be a most beautiful impulse in itself. But beware of the dinosaur lurking behind the rose bush.

The St Valentine's Day tradition started in the time of the Roman Empire, where 14 February was a holiday to honour Juno, patroness of women and of marriage and queen of Roman Gods and Goddesses. It was also the eve of the festival of Lupercalia where, amidst a variety of other ceremonies, the names of young women were placed in a box, from which they were drawn by young men. Drawing a girl's name would make you partners for the festival. Sometimes the pairing lasted an entire year, and would often lead to marriage. As with other pagan feast days, it was the strategy of the Christian church to adopt and baptise these already existing celebrations. The strictly pagan elements in these feasts were baptised by substituting the names of saints for those of the Roman Gods and Goddesses. And so, gradually, 14 February became the date for exchanging love messages and St Valentine became the patron saint of lovers in the Roman Church.

But why St Valentine? Emperor Claudius II (268-270) involved in many bloody and unpopular wars, found it difficult to recruit soldiers for his army. He decided that Roman men had become too soft and domesticated to leave their families. So he cancelled all marriages and betrothals. Valentine, a priest in Rome in those days, secretly married couples, for which he was apprehended, dragged before the Prefect and condemned to death. Legend has it that he left a farewell note for the jailer's daughter, who had become his friend, and signed it 'From Your Valentine,' unknowingly sending the first Valentine Card on 14 February 270. It was in 496 that Pope Gelasius made this his feastday.

However, the dinosaur here being described, owes more to a Miss Esther Howland in the United States of America about fifteen hundred years later, who is credited with sending the first commercial Valentine Card. She launched the avalanche of valentine cards which the stationary industry dinosaur introduced in the 1800s. Loveland, Colorado, holds the record for the largest post office business in the world around 14 February each year.

As for St Valentine himself, not too many people know that he, or at least parts of him, is buried in Ireland, where a church in Dublin, built in the 19th century, became his final resting place. In 1835 Pope Gregory XVI (1831-1846) gave these relics to an Irish Carmelite preaching in Rome. A reliquary containing the remains of St Valentine arrived in Dublin and was brought in solemn procession to Whitefriar Street Church, where an altar and shrine are visited by lovers ever since.

Finally, why roses? The rose appears in the earliest traditions of poetry and art as a favourite flower. Sacred to Aphrodite, it was used medically – Pliny lists thirty-two remedies from its petals and leaves – before becoming a universal symbol. It more recently became the emblem of England and the national flower of the United States. And here the dinosaur takes over: the estimated number of roses produced for St Valentine's Day, as recorded in the first decade of this twenty-first century, is 187 million per year. California produces sixty per cent of American roses, but the vast number sold on Valentine's Day are imported from South America. Sixty percent of these come from Columbia which is the second-largest exporter of cut flowers after the Netherlands – where our first MNA dinosaur came from.

This globalised dinosaur plant pits its interests against the cheap labour of poorer countries. Employment is seventy per cent of the product cost. If the workers refuse to co-operate with the level of production required, or if they demand higher wages, then our carnivorous bipedal develops wings and become a pterodactyl, flying to wherever the tax bait is richer and the labour hire cheaper. China looks like a good career move at present.

Many dinosaurs, as we have learned, build nests and lay eggs! And this can happen anywhere in the world where the workforce is pliable. The major difference between reptiles and mammals is in the way they reproduce themselves. Mammals carry their young inside their bodies until these develop sufficiently to be born into the world. Reptiles lay eggs and their young eventually hatch on their own. Mammals develop an attachment to their offspring and are inclined to look after and defend them. Not so the dinosaurs, who lay their eggs and walk away cold-bloodedly, leaving their young to fend for themselves. (The second part of our brain turns us into over-obsessive parents. Dinosaurs, who rely on the reptilian brain have no such hang-ups.)

In the dinosaur plant, more than 100,000 workers help grow, sort, and package $1 billion worth of flowers in Columbia every year. Such productivity requires painful, low-paid labour by a largely female workforce. Women work from 6.00 am to 10.00 pm every day. In the greenhouses where there are 700-800 flowers per bed, conditions are perfect for roses but lethal for humans. Temperatures are hot and the atmosphere is poisonous. Each worker is required to cut 300 flowers per hour. The repetitive task of cutting stems of flowers with a secateurs for such long hours causes painful trapped tendon injuries. Workers complain about lack of protective equipment and clothing. They are exposed to pesticides and fungicides. Such chemicals cause headaches, asthma, nausea, and impaired vision. But this work is the only kind available and their only source of income. Without these roses Columbians are destitute. If they complain too forcibly the dinosaur will fly elsewhere.

'Flowers for the Gringo'[2] the workers call the roses. Unless these are a certain length and standard of perfection, as dictated by the starry-eyed lovers from the richer countries, they are rejected by the buyers. Grading of roses comes before and after the harvest. There are three categories: Grade 1, a tight rose bud; Grade 2, a semi-open bud; Grade 3, the full-blown rose. America, apparently, has a love affair with Grade 1, the 'rose bud,' even though this is the hardest to guarantee as a later full-blown rose. Ironically the 'blown rose,' rejected by every buyer, is, in fact, the flower as nature intended it. But try telling that to the bud-guzzling dinosaur!

The word 'Gringo' comes from a song, based on a poem of Robbie Burns, 'Green Grow the Rushes Oh!' British soldiers frequently sang it as they marched. The first two words (*Green Grow = Gringo*) became the soldiers' signature in South America and Mexico. The workers sing the dinosaur's song without even understanding the words.

* * *

---

2. cf *Flowers for the Gringo*, What in the World?, 2009, Kmf DVD, Series 4, www.kmfproductions.net

Why would any such dinosaurs come to Ireland? And why would they stay here? More recent variations of the song 'Galway Bay' may hold a clue:

> Now the breezes blowing o'er the seas from Ireland
> Are perfumed by the heather as they blow
> Enticing strangers everywhere to Ireland
> For more than leprechauns and mistletoe.

Ireland's low corporate tax rate of 12.5% on trading profits has been a magnet for MNC dinosaurs who, in turn, represent 90% of Irish exports. Between 1998 and 2002, profits of US companies with Irish facilities doubled. Even in the present monetary crisis, figures released in September 2010 for exports from Ireland, exceeded €40 billion in the April-June period, a record figure for a single quarter, topping the previous high water mark reached in the final three months of 2008.

The first dinosaur sighted in Ireland in the last quarter of the twentieth century still lives in a cave, now world famous for its stalagmites and stalactites, at Ringaskiddy. Pfizer was the first MNC dinosaur to migrate to Ireland, raising its leg and pouring citric acid over County Cork from 1969. With headquarters in New York, Pfizer is the world's largest biopharmaceutical company, and one of Ireland's leading employers. It manufactures here some of its best-selling medicines including *Lipitor* and *Viagra*.

Viagra is known locally as the 'Pfizer riser,' while Lipitor is its great 'down-sizer'. Viagra, the first of the Pfizer twin towers, is probably the most famous product of the twentieth century, as well as being the most wanted and least needed in pharmaceutical history. Lipitor comes hot on its heels. At least sixteen million people in America take drugs to reduce cholesterol. I myself am one of the adults who have taken it every evening for the last five years. This is to lower my bad cholesterol when I know full well that a low fat diet and other non-medical treatments, such as daily exercise and lifestyle changes, would do the job quite as effectively. But who am I to turn down that double whopper McDonald's cheese burger with Ireland's favourite Hellmann's real mayonnaise on top, when I can now have heaven and all this as well by taking my daily dose of Lipitor?

Although there are other dinosaurs out there, ready and able to flood the market with LDL (so-called bad cholesterol-reducing commodities), the Pfizer dinosaur maintains its monopoly and mutilates or destroys all rivals. It recently gobbled up Wyeth in a $68 billion takeover deal.

The Lipitor battle has become a test of the pharmaceutical industry's ability to defend name brands. Even as insurance companies, patients and doctors, seek to lessen the world's billion dollar annual prescription drug bill, by using generic alternatives whenever possible, no generic version of Lipitor is in the offing because the US Patent and Trademark Office reissued to Pfizer a patent that expires in June 2011. As I write this book, Pfizer remains the only provider of this drug to an ever expanding number of the world's population. It has succeeded in lowering the age-group to expand its catchment area further. On 7 July 2010, EC approval was issued for a new chewable type of Lipitor which can be used by ten-year-old children. Now if, as we are told, there are nearly seven billion people on the planet, then the goal presumably is to get as many of these as possible chewing Lipitor every day at several dollars a crunch.

The first home-grown dinosaur in Ireland was introduced by Tony Ryan (1936-2007), then an Aer Lingus executive. A co-founder of Ryanair, Tony built this country's biggest business [GPA], a commercial aircraft sales and leasing company in 1975. At its peak, it was valued at $4 billion net income and reached $265 million in the year to 31st March 1992. Enter Ireland's dinosaur number three.

The GPA group set its sights on a major stock market flotation. Here was a company expected to grow phenomenally. It was to be a super stock, with GPA expected to account for one-fifth of the entire market value of the Irish Exchange. There was to be a simultaneous mid-summer launch in London, New York, Tokyo and Dublin. Great pride and confidence in Irish investor and media circles were, unfortunately, not shared in bigger money markets, where the even larger dinosaurs roam. Concerns were growing about the cyclical nature of demand for aircraft. International stock markets were jittery in the early 1990s and then there was The Gulf War (August 2, 1990-February 28, 1991). Lack of investor enthusiasm, and disagreement over the appropriate launch price, led to the failure of the flotation. Within a year, Guinness Peat Aviation was in serious trouble.

The (GECAS) dinosaur was waiting in the wings. GE Capital Aviation Services is the largest owner/lessor of commercial aircraft in the world and is part of the US General Electric Company. It established a base in Shannon (its largest operational centre outside of the US) in 1993. It has over 1,800 owned and managed aircraft, twenty-four offices, and more than 270 customers in over seventy-five countries. *Céad míle fáilte* and *ad multos annos* to the GECAS Dinosaur, going forward, as we say!

* * *

Every century seems to begin with a spectacular event which heralds the shape of the history to follow. The sinking of the *Titanic*, that largest of all dinosaurs afloat at that time, traumatised the century to follow and presaged the carnage of mechanised warfare which characterised the twentieth century. In the last years of that century, one of the largest audiences ever watched the film *Titanic*, which was launched in 1997 and made $1.8 billion at the box-office, with around 390-400 million tickets sold worldwide. DVD sales and rentals brought in another $1.2 billion, meaning that between sixty and a hundred million people bought the DVD or rented it, and numbers keep growing as viewers are still watching. All in all, one could estimate that around 500 million people saw this film. So for a hundred years since 14 April 1912, the sinking of the *Titanic* has been on our psychic radar screens. It became a theme of our collective nightmare.

Similarly, the fall of the Twin Towers on 9/11, 2001 has become a symbol of the dinosaur wars at the beginning of our twenty-first century. The battle between 'The Skyscraper and the Airplane'[3] could only have taken place in this twenty-first century. Monster skyscraper buildings could not have happened unless the century which produced them also invented cheap high-quality structural steel. This was the first revolutionary architectural invention since the Romans created the arch

---

3. Adam Goodheart, 'The Skyscraper and the Airplane', *The American Scholar*, published by the Phi Beta Kappa Society, vol 71, No 1, Winter 2002, p 17f

and the dome two millennia previously. Buildings now became vertebrates rather than awkward crustaceans: they could stand slender and tall without huge carapaces of supporting masonry. 176,000 tons of fabricated structural steel was a landmark in welding history. The combination of express and local elevator banks, called a skylobby system, was one of the ways in which the architect advanced the art of building through the potential of modern technology. The other previous, less flamboyant but equally important, inventions of the twentieth century were electric lighting, central heating, fire escapes, telephones and flush toilets. We had created the Meccano set with which to construct our idiosyncratic dinosaur.

Neither could the felling of the Twin Towers have occurred much before 9/11, 2001. A Boeing 707, the largest plane flying when the twin towers were planned, was catered for and would have been absorbable had it hit either tower. The excursion monitor on the roof of the towers did not even register in 1993 when a truck bomb was detonated beneath the North Tower. The explosion at that time was intended to knock the North Tower (Tower One) into the South Tower (Tower Two), bringing both towers down and killing thousands of people. It failed to do so, although it did kill six people and injured over a thousand. The world had to wait for the invention of the Boeing 767 to achieve this goal.

According to Stanford University Professor Steven Block,[4] the energy generated by a fuel-laden Boeing 757 or 767, colliding into a World Trade Centre tower, is roughly equivalent to one-twentieth of the energy of the atomic bomb dropped on Hiroshima. Ignited fuel generated 90% of the energy in the explosion. A Boeing 767's fuel capacity is roughly 23,980 gallons, and a Boeing 757 carries roughly 11,466 gallons. The terrorists intentionally took over planes scheduled to travel across the country because they'd be carrying more fuel and would therefore cause more devastation on impact.

The 767 twin-engined jumbo jet had been put into service

---

4. Block is a professor of applied physics and biological sciences and an expert on national security and terrorism. He spoke at a press conference on the afternoon of September 11th as reported by Jennifer Deitz Berry in *Palo Alto Weekly* Online Edition, 4.pm 11/09/2001

nineteen years before 11 September 2001. Both these dinosaurs, therefore, the skyscraper and the aeroplane, had been brought to the pitch of refinement which allowed one of them to become the deadly weapon of destruction for the other. Neither could have achieved the kind of insertion and implosion, which wreaked such total havoc, before our twenty-first century. Science and technology take a bow.

One of the ironies of architecture is that Minoru Yamasaki, who designed the World Trade Centre, suffered from vertigo and was afraid of heights. He once wrote that in a world of perfect freedom he would have created nothing but one-storey buildings overlooking fields of flowers. However, the brief presented to him was quite explicit: 12 million square feet of floor area on a sixteen acre site and a budget of $500 million.

The next time the dinosaurs are wiped out, it may not be owing to a meteor from outside. It may be the result of internal combustion.

Now don't get me wrong. I'm not saying that we in Ireland, for instance, are unhappy about having the Pfizer plant in Ringaskiddy. On the contrary, we are delighted, especially in view of the closure of several other such sites throughout the country. What I am saying is that you who work for such dinosaurs, on whatever floor of the skyscraper, would do well to study the species in depth and in detail so that you learn how to dance without doing serious damage to yourselves.

* * *

On 7 August 1974, Philip Pettit, French acrobat and tight-rope walker, threw a wire between the twin towers in Manhattan, which were over 1,360 feet high, and walked the sixty metres distance between them for forty minutes carrying a light aluminium pole to give himself balance. His dance with these two dinosaurs changed their profile as sombre geopolitical symbols into elegant footholds for one crazy acrobat. Like the fool in some medieval court, he put a smile on the frowning face of the sauropod. We have to take our cue from him and learn the secret of walking the tight-rope between the Brachiosaurid breed of dinosaur. These latter, like our skyscrapers, were the tallest on record. Their front legs were longer than their rear legs, giving them a giraffe-like stance. Their long necks, held vertically, allowed for grazing among the tallest trees. *Brachiosaurus*, the best known of the group, was thirteen metres tall. *Sauroposeidon* eventually grew to 18.5 metres, making it the tallest of all.

Let the Great World Spin, Colum McCann suggests, in his novel[5] about New York. We can't help living in a spinning galaxy of potentially destructive monsters, but we mustn't allow ourselves to get caught in the whirling. Let the great world spin, certainly, because there is nothing much we can do about it, but learn, like Philip Pettit, to do the tight-rope dance between the towers. Don't let yourself be smashed to pieces as Pettit's *Doppelgänger* in the novel, Fr Corrigan, was, looking for his equilibrium in more dangerous places. Between the feet of the dinosaur, McCann's novel offers a portrait of the average citizen of New York. 'Park Avenue socialites, Bronx junkies, Centre Street judges, downtown artists and their subway-tagging counterparts, street priests, weary cops, wearier hookers, grieving mothers of an Asian war, form the underbelly of the society which watches a pin-dot of a man walking on air 110 stories above their heads (Richard Price, reviewing this book).' The watchers were essentially divided into two camps: those who secretly wanted to see the tightrope walker fall, prefiguring what the towers held in store – to 'see someone arc downward all that distance, to disappear from the sight line, flail, smash to the ground and give the Wednesday an electricity, a meaning' – and those who 'wanted the man to save himself, step backward into the arms of the cops instead of the sky'. Corrigan, too, watches this display of human possibility and the next day he loses his nerve, brakes at the wrong moment on the freeway, is clipped by the car behind him and is parachuted towards destruction along with his passenger in the car. In the second before their death both Corrigan and his passenger, Jazzlyn, a young prostitute in a Day-Glo swimsuit, experience a kind of weightlessness akin to that of the tight-rope walker for the first and only time in their lives. Corrigan is based, according to the author, on Philip Francis Berrigan (1923-2002), an internationally

---

5. Colum McCann, *Let The Great World Spin,* New York, Random House, 2009.

renowned American Christian Peace Activist, and former
Roman Catholic priest. The novel is told by the older brother
who comes to America from Ireland to find his sibling 'like he
was some bright hallelujah in the shitbox of what the world really was.' Daniel Berrigan, Catholic Priest, Jesuit poet and peace
activist, is Philip Berrigan's older brother in real life. But, the
novel suggests, the younger missioner to the Bronx, like
Dostoevsky's Idiot, never learned to dance with the dinosaurs
and was eventually crushed at their feet.

PART TWO

Descent from the Dinosasur

Snake by D. H. Lawrence
A snake came to my water-trough
On a hot, hot day, and I in pyjamas for the heat,
To drink there.

In the deep, strange-scented shade of the great dark carob-
tree
I came down the steps with my pitcher
And must wait, must stand and wait, for there he was at the
trough before me.
He reached down from a fissure in the earth-wall in the
gloom
And trailed his yellow-brown slackness soft-bellied down,
over the edge of the stone trough
And rested his throat upon the stone bottom,
And where the water had dripped from the tap, in a small
clearness,
He sipped with his straight mouth,
Softly drank through his straight gums, into his slack long
body,
Silently.

Someone was before me at my water-trough,
And I, like a second comer, waiting.

He lifted his head from his drinking, as cattle do,
And looked at me vaguely, as drinking cattle do,
And flickered his two-forked tongue from his lips, and
mused a moment,
And stooped and drank a little more,
Being earth-brown, earth-golden from the burning bowels of
the earth
On the day of Sicilian July, with Etna smoking.

The voice of my education said to me
He must be killed,
For in Sicily the black, black snakes are innocent, the gold are
venomous.

And voices in me said, If you were a man
You would take a stick and break him now, and finish him
off.

But must I confess how I liked him,
How glad I was he had come like a guest in quiet, to drink at
my water-trough
And depart peaceful, pacified, and thankless,
Into the burning bowels of this earth?

Was it cowardice, that I dared not kill him?
Was it perversity, that I longed to talk to him?
Was it humility, to feel so honoured?

I felt so honoured.
And yet those voices:
If you were not afraid, you would kill him!

And truly I was afraid, I was most afraid,
But even so, honoured still more
That he should seek my hospitality
From out the dark door of the secret earth.
He drank enough
And lifted his head, dreamily, as one who has drunken,
And flickered his tongue like a forked night on the air, so black;
Seeming to lick his lips,
And looked around like a god, unseeing, into the air,
And slowly turned his head,
And slowly, very slowly, as if thrice adream,
Proceeded to draw his slow length curving round
And climb again the broken bank of my wall-face.

And as he put his head into that dreadful hole,
And as he slowly drew up, snake-easing his shoulders, and
entered farther,
A sort of horror, a sort of protest against his withdrawing
into that horrid black hole,

Deliberately going into the blackness, and slowly drawing
himself after,
Overcame me now his back was turned.

I looked round, I put down my pitcher,
I picked up a clumsy log
And threw it at the water-trough with a clatter.

I think it did not hit him,
But suddenly that part of him that was left behind convulsed
in undignified haste.
Writhed like lightning, and was gone
Into the black hole, the earth-lipped fissure in the wall-front,
At which, in the intense still noon, I stared with fascination.

And immediately I regretted it.
I thought how paltry, how vulgar, what a mean act!
I despised myself and the voices of my accursed human
education.

And I thought of the albatross
And I wished he would come back, my snake.

For he seemed to me again like a king,
Like a king in exile, uncrowned in the underworld,
Now due to be crowned again.

And so, I missed my chance with one of the lords
Of life.
And I have something to expiate:
A pettiness.

Born by nature and biology to go the horizontal path from
birth through copulation to death, humanity is called to take the
vertical option and rise from the dead. 'I will put enmity between you and the woman, and between your offspring and
hers.' The great divide between the serpents and the mammals
was precisely in terms of their offspring. As we split off from the
reptilian line, 'a fresh neural structure blossomed within our
skulls. This brand-new brain transformed not just the mechanics
of reproduction but also the organismic *orientation* toward offspring.' The reptile lays its eggs and slithers away indifferently.
The mammal nourishes and safeguards its young from the hostile

world outside its group.[1] But such a change in orientation shifted the balance of our make-up. We had to produce more head room to accommodate the new growth taking place in our brains. The continuing development of ourselves as human beings, which now becomes our inherited make-up, had a great deal to do with our decision at some point on the evolutionary trajectory to stand up straight on our hind legs and walk tall. This changed everything about us, not simply our posture. We became vertical.

As a result of this move upwards we had to double our brain space and develop such outsized heads that if they were to be allowed to mature fully in the womb it would be impossible to give birth to them. Because we happened to stand up some thousands of years ago and walk on our hind legs, something changed in our centre of gravity and as a consequence the most extraordinary growth occurred in our metabolism: we developed a larger brain. This required a massive redistribution of body weight and the net result, for the rest of our history as a species, is that our heads became too big. The brain needs such extensive head room that we now have to wait until we are outside the womb to allow its extensive accommodation to develop fully. To allow this to happen we have to be born before our time. We have to emerge from the womb before our heads have developed to that full capacity which would prevent us from exiting from the restricted escape route which nature has provided in the bodies of our mothers to negotiate our release.

Our first step on the road to resurrection was to stop crawling along the ground and stand up. Once this had happened we changed our orientation and began to develop organs which would cope, not only with the newer and higher aerial view, but also with the revolution in social sensitisation which this massive shift of emphasis installed. We are no longer simply yours truly crawling indifferently in horizontal search for sustenance and survival, we have developed a further brain structure which made us altruistic at the same time as it doubled the size of our heads. But such a highly complex interplay with our envir-

---

1. *A General Theory of Love*, Thomas Lewis MD, Fari Amini MD, Richard Lannon MD, Vintage Books, New York, 2000, p 25

onment takes more time to mature. In the first seven years, a child learns to sense its body and the world around it and to rise up and move effectively in that world. The human brain is the product of 500 million years of evolution in vertebrate animals. Vertebrates are animals with a backbone. This privilege is shared by us with fish, dogs, and monkeys for instance. All vertebrates have a central nervous system – a spinal cord and a brain – in which sensations come together and responses originate. A jellyfish is an example of an invertebrate that has nerve cells but no central nervous system and, therefore, little capacity to integrate sensations. Such primitive fish were the ancestors both of modern fish, of amphibians, of reptiles, birds, mammals and ourselves.

The first structures and functions of the brain which developed have not changed very much. These we share with our reptilian ancestors. But as the brain evolved, new structures and functions were added to these basic elements. The older parts continue to function today in much the same way as they did for our ancestors millions of years ago. But we have developed two more storeys onto this basic primordial structure. Although the primitive part remains active and true to itself, our total being is transformed by the two other layers which have been placed over this, while at the same time remaining interconnected. Essentially our topmost brain is a versatile fixture. Not only can it influence the other two parts of itself but it can develop itself and become transformed by whatever intentionality we have towards surpassing ourselves. Whatever we want to be, whatever we decide to be, is what we can become. The ambidexterity and subtlety of our more developed brain structure allows for all such possibility. We can determine our own future.

We only have to examine nature as it displays itself around us to see the similarities and the differences between ourselves and the other mammals. Horses, cattle and sheep, for example, stand up and walk on perfectly formed limbs within minutes of their birth. We, on the other hand, are premature babies whose most characteristic organ, our brain, is only fractionally developed when we land on the earth. We arrive in the world as underdeveloped foetuses. Unlike the foals, calves, and lambs that arrive each spring fully made-up and ready to roll, we do not have the complete set on the day we are born, we have to grow into ourselves.

When you think how consistent and powerful gravity is, you realise how much inner drive the child must have to rise to a standing position in just one year. This standing up alone is one of the biggest events in early childhood. It is the end product of all the integration of gravity, movement, muscle and joint sensations of the months before. A relatively tall body must balance itself on two tiny feet. The months which precede this event are arduous and painstaking.

After we learn to hold our head up with our neck muscles, we use the muscles of our upper back and arms to lift our chests off the floor. Most of us adopt what is referred to as 'the aeroplane position' after six months, which involves lying face downwards in 'the prone extension posture' (the natural posture of the snake), where we balance our whole body on our stomachs making us look a bit like an aeroplane. Such is the vital action in developing the muscles used for rolling over, standing up, and walking. The so-called 'neck righting reflex,' a result of interplay between the forces of gravity and the muscles and joints of the neck, taking place ever since birth, helps us to turn over from our backs to our stomachs. This is the same reflex we share with other mammals. It is the one which proverbially allows the cat to land always on its feet. The gravity receptors which allow us to pit ourselves so dexterously or pedestrianly against the forces of nature are located in our inner ears. All of which development, if successfully completed, allows locomotion to take place between six to eight months.[2] It takes us much longer than horses and calves to hit the tarmac running, as they say, because our locomotion is a more complicated and sophisticated operation, carrying within it the seeds of a much more demanding flight-path.

'Babies are born with a brain that is one quarter of the size of their adult brain. In a sense, compared to other species human babies are born prematurely in that they have a very long period of complete reliance on their primary caregiver (usually the

2. A. Jean Ayers, *Sensory Integration and the Child*, WPS, Los Angeles, 1979 [Fourteenth Printing, 2000] p 18-20

mother) for their survival.'[3] The positive side to all this is that
we are the only creatures who can determine what we want to
become. We can remain prisoners to our DNA (as are animals,
birds, bees) or we can break out and take off in another direction. The notion that we are born to be inescapably selfish, that
our instincts and habits are too deeply ingrained to be eradicated,
that we are biologically determined and victims of a precoded
system which dictates our behavioural responses, is belied by
recent scientific research.

What is called the 'constructionist view' of evolution suggests that we are not only capable of changing ourselves and our
environment but we are biologically built to do so, and our instinct is towards growth of unimaginable variety. Far from
being predetermined either by our environment or our genes,
we are provided with an adaptive plasticity which awaits our
decisive action before it forms us into the eventual shape we
choose to become. This means that we are not hardwired by our
hormones towards addictive infatuation, for instance. At the
level of breathing, sneezing, swallowing, our reactions are
genetically determined, but 'at higher levels, where learning occurs, an entirely new principle of organisation comes into being.
These areas are uncommitted at birth, and their development
depends on the particularities of life experience: they assume a
function in the course of life.'[4]

In other words, the shape of who we are as human beings
emerges under the influence of what we believe, what we want
and what we experience. 'There is a concept called Brain
Plasticity – meaning that you can mould the brain, or the brain is
changeable, especially early in life. For example, when we learn
new things, our brain is changing. During development, first,
cells are made. Then the cells move to specific areas in the brain.

---

3. Dr Stuart Shanker is a Distinguished Research Professor of
Philosophy and Psychology at York University and currently serving
as Director of the Milton and Ethel Harris Research Initiative (MEHRI),
an initiative whose goal is to build on new knowledge of the brain's development, and help set children (including those with developmental
disorders) on the path towards emotional and intellectual health.
4. Oliver Sacks, 'Scotoma: Forgetting and Neglect in Science' in *Hidden
Histories of Science*, ed B. Silvers, London 1997, pp 176-7

Each cell then changes into a specific brain cell (neuron), with a specific function. The different neurons make connections with other cells. Over time plasticity decreases, meaning it is harder, but not impossible, to develop new connections between brain cells. As brains develop, there are millions of connections made and then those that aren't needed are discarded.'[5]

Evolution occurs according to the direction or intentionality towards which humanity strains. Limbs drop off as they become redundant; others sprout or change shape and texture, to adjust to the task, the environment, the purpose. Scales become skin; fins become wings. Our hands become claws, fingers, fists, or they become delicate wings, depending upon how or what we decide to touch.

Our sense of touch operates fairly well for several months in the womb. However, in that situation we cannot tell very well where we are being touched, because our brains cannot yet differentiate one spot from another. In the first month every human baby will automatically grasp any object that touches the palm of its hand. This reflex is designed to help the child to hang onto something so that they don't fall. Because the newborn does not have the ability to open or extend their fingers, their hands often remain curled into loose fists for the first few months of life. These are our reptilian reflexes which evolved in our serpentine ancestors, who needed them for infant survival. Evolution occurs very slowly and nature does not readily give up a form of behaviour that has served survival for millions of years.[6] Yet we have to recognise these automatic reactions for what they are and train them to accommodate themselves to our new altruistic state of being, which requires of us to be less selfishly grasping. This takes time. For the normal three-month-old child, grasping is still an automatic reaction. We cannot voluntarily release our hold on whatever comes within reach of our hands until we have learned to coordinate the parts of our brain that are able to 'see' with those parts that 'feel'. By the time the

5. R. C. Lewontin, 'Genes, Environment and Organisms' in *Hidden Histories of Science*, ed B. Silvers, London 1997, p 136
6. A. Jean Ayers, *Sensory Integration and the Child*, WPS, Los Angeles, 1979 [Fourteenth Printing, 2000] p 15

child is eight years old, this touch system is almost as mature as it will ever be.

Dr Paul MacLean (1913-2007), an evolutionary neuroanatomist and senior research scientist at the Yale Medical School and the National Institute of Mental Health in the United States, has argued that the human brain is comprised of three distinct sub-brains, each the product of a separate age in evolutionary history.[7] The trio intermingles and communicates, but some information is inevitably lost in translation because the subunits differ in their functions, properties, and even their chemistries. The oldest or reptilian brain is a bulbous elaboration of the spinal cord. This brain, which we inherit directly from the dinosaurs, 'houses vital control centres – neurons that prompt breathing, swallowing, and heartbeat, and the visual tracking system a frog relies on to snap a dancing dragonfly out of the air. The startle centre is here, too, because a swift reaction to abrupt movement or noise is the principal reason animals have brains at all.'[8]

Steeped in the physiology of survival, the reptilian brain is the one still functioning in a person who is 'brain-dead'. If the reptilian brain dies, the rest of the body will follow; the other two brains are less essential to the neurology of sustaining life [22]. The reptilian brain permits rudimentary interactions: displays of aggression and courtship, mating and territorial defence [23]. This antediluvian brain has motivations more suited to the lives of asocial carnivores, which this brain was designed to serve.

The limbic system (or Paleomammalian brain) is a set of brain structures which, according to MacLean, form the inner border of the cortex (*limbus* is the Latin word for 'border' or 'edge'). Although there is much disagreement about the exact

7. P. D. MacLean, *A Triune Concept of the Brain and Behavior*, Toronto, University of Toronto Press, 1973; *The Triune Brain in Evolution*, New York, Plenum Press, 1990
8. *A General Theory of Love*, Thomas Lewis MD, Fari Amini MD, Richard Lannon MD, Vintage Books, New York, 2000. This book gives a summary of more scientific research in the area. For the remainder of this section I shall refer to this work with the page number in a square bracket.

function of each of these three aspects of the triune brain, this second part seems more adapted to our emotional life. MacLean referred to it as 'the visceral brain' in a paper he wrote in 1952. This 'emotional' brain, though inarticulate and unreasoning, can be expressive and intuitive [34]. It also seems to be responsible for turning us into over-obsessive parents. Dinosaurs, who rely on the reptilian brain only, have no such hang-ups about their offspring.

Moving towards the later brain, which is where we can express ourselves in clear-cut abstract fashion, is often a difficult and frustrating passage. And so people must strain to force a strong feeling into the straitjacket of verbal expression. Poetry, a bridge between the neocortical and limbic brains, begins, according to Robert Frost, 'as a lump in the throat, a sense of wrong, a homesickness, a love sickness. It is never a thought to begin with.'

The newest brain (*neocortex* – Greek for 'new' and Latin for 'rind' or 'bark') is the last and, in humans, the largest of the three brains. Mammals like the opossum which evolved long ago have only a thin skin of neo-cortex. Dogs and cats have more, and monkeys, more still. In human beings, the neocortex has ballooned to massive proportions. Human beings have the largest neo-cortex-to-brain ratio of any creature, an inequitable proportion that confers upon us our capacity to reason. The jurisdiction of will is also limited to this latest brain and to those functions within its purview [33].

It may be helpful to picture the human neocortex as two symmetrical sheets, each the size of a large, thick linen napkin, and each crumpled for better cramming into the small oblate shell of the skull [27].

So, this 'triune' brain is what we are dealing with when we talk about dancing with the dinosaur which is still within ourselves. The authors of this book, from which I am quoting extensively, take great pains to stress that evolution is a random process that does not proceed in an orderly fashion. Evolution is 'a kaleidoscope, not a pyramid'. They warn us against buying into a simplistic version of a most mysterious and complex system. 'Many people conceive of evolution as an upward staircase, an unfolding sequence that produces ever more advanced organisms [30].' This also prevents us from either overemphasising the importance of the latest version or dismissing or undervaluing the everpresent reptilian component of the brain. 'The neocortical brain is not the most advanced of the three, but simply the most recent.' We need all three components and our dance involves the correct balance and appropriate weight afforded to each one of the three. Because the three are designed to interrelate. 'Each brain has evolved to interdigitate with its cranial cohabitants [31].' These authors find the complication and confusion of our triune brain as confirmation of its haphazard appearance. 'Thus the development of the human brain was neither planned nor seamlessly executed. It simply happened.'

For my part, I find the very triune structure of the brain, which they so clearly and articulately describe, the most convincing proof of the handiwork of God, almost like the signature of the Trinity. And so I also look to the so-called 'perichoresis' which describes the intermingling and interconnection between the three persons of the Trinity, as a template for the way in which we have to allow each of the three parts of our brain to be assumed into the final shape of it, which we are able to induce because of the plasticity and malleability of its third incarnation in the neocortex and because of the prompting of the Holy Spirit.

If we plan to reach out towards infinity and live for eternity we need to make some adjustments to our life patterns here on earth. Even if we were to take a trip to Mars, for example, we would be exposed to reduced or zero gravity for up to three years. We would have to learn how to exercise and train our bodies not only to survive such a trip but also to be fit on arrival. Because when we land on the red planet three years later, we would have to be strong enough to walk and to work.

Most astronauts in our short experience were men and it took until the twenty-first century to secure a proportionality of one woman for every five of them. Women training for this journey into space had to undergo a strange ordeal. They had to spend sixty days in bed supervised by CCT cameras to ensure that they never got up. This experience would prepare them for outer space. They lounged on hospital beds tilted so their feet were six degrees higher than their heads. This longterm position provoked a physical reaction akin to weightlessness. In space, as in off-kilter beds, fluids shift to the upper body, which can make the face swell, disrupt digestion and bring on vertigo. Astronauts have to learn how to cope with such extra-terrestrial demands on the human body. In other words, even such re-arrangements of gravity require an effort of bodily adjustment which those interested in the adventure have to make. Interestingly, from the point of view of evolution, one authority has suggested that in microgravity human beings become halfway between a fish and a bird.

PART THREE

The Church as Dinosaur

From the Book of Genesis to the Book of Revelation, the first and last books of the Christian Bible, the serpent is portrayed as the symbol of evil.

A great portent appeared in heaven: a woman clothed with the sun, with the moon under her feet, and on her head a crown of twelve stars. She was pregnant and was crying out in birth pangs, and in the agony of giving birth. And there was seen another sign in heaven. Then another portent appeared in heaven: a great red dragon, with seven heads and ten horns and seven diadems on his heads. His tail swept down a third of the stars of heaven and threw them to the earth. Then the dragon stood before the woman who was about to bear a child, so that he might devour her child as soon as it was born. And she gave birth to a son, a male child, who is to rule all the nations with a rod of iron. But her child was snatched away and taken to God and to his throne, and the woman fled into the wilderness, where she has a place prepared by God, so that there she can be nourished for one thousand two hundred and sixty days.

And war broke out in heaven: Michael and his angels fought against the dragon. The dragon and his angels fought back, but they were defeated, and there was no longer any place for them in heaven. The great dragon was thrown down, that ancient serpent, who is called the Devil and Satan, the deceiver of the whole world – he was thrown down to the earth, and his angels were thrown down with him.

And I heard a loud voice in heaven, saying: Now have come the salvation and the power and the kingdom of our God and the authority of his Messiah, for the accuser of our comrades has been thrown down, who accuses them day and night before our God. But they have conquered him by the blood of the Lamb and by the word of their testimony, for they cling not to life even in the face of death. Rejoice then , you heavens and those who dwell in them! But woe to the earth and the sea, for the devil has come down to you with great wrath, because he knows that his time is short.

So when the dragon saw that he had been thrown down to the earth, he pursued the woman who had given birth to the male child. But the woman was given the two wings of a great eagle, so that she could fly from the serpent into the wilderness, to her place where she is nourished for a time and times, and half a time. The from his mouth the serpent poured water like a river after the woman, to sweep her away with the flood. But the earth came to the help of the woman; it opened its mouth and swallowed the river that the dragon poured from his mouth. Then the dragon was angry with the woman, and went off to make war on the rest of her children, those who keep the commandments of God and hold the testimony of Jesus Christ. Then the dragon took his stand on the sand of the seashore.[1]

As has been pointed out, every large institution that means to survive on this planet has to become a dinosaur. The Catholic Church (The Greek word καθολικός (*katholikos*) means 'universal') has over one billion members living in almost every country in the world and is the oldest religious institution in existence. So, the Roman Catholic Church inevitably became a dinosaur, in its institutional aspect, over the 2,000 years of its existence.

Although this time span is short when compared with the history of the universe, it is still significant in terms of our human history. It began in Jerusalem with a small nucleus of disciples who believed in the resurrection of Jesus. *The Acts of the Apostles* suggests and describes how this small group lived the Christian life as it was intended to be. The 'Council' of Jerusalem, which took place at some time between 48 and 52AD, became a defining moment. Christianity officially broke away from the Jewish tradition and reached out to all people regard-

---

1. Revelation 12:1-18

less of race, language, or cultural background. The gain from this was universality; the loss was essential rootedness in Judaism.

In the beginning, the followers of Jesus lived as Jews, participated in Jewish worship, and observed ancient Jewish law. When the young Christian Church spread east to Antioch, where the name 'Christian' was first invented, the words 'the Catholic Church' (ἡ καθολικὴ ἐκκλησία) appeared in a letter from the bishop of Antioch, the bishop and martyr Ignatius, written to Christians in Smyrna in the year 107.

The apostle Paul (c.5-c.67AD), was not, as these dates suggest, a contemporary of Jesus even though he became one of those most responsible for the spread of Christianity. He received a special revelation which he claimed was of the risen Christ, in 37AD after the martyrdom of St Stephen, the first Christian to be put to death for his faith in Jesus. Paul's version of Christianity was questioned by others from the very beginning as it has been ever since. He was accused of corrupting and complicating the simple message. His dramatic conversion from being a persecuting Jew seemed to influence the way in which he viewed Christianity as a religion of redemption and as essentially opposed to Judaism.

Many scholars agree that Pauline theology has a different look and feel to that of the synoptic gospels. However, most would deny that Paul's is a betrayal of the Christian gospel; rather they accept that there is a 'development' from Jesus of Nazareth to Paul of Tarsus, and that this development is the work of the Holy Spirit, which characterises also the history of Christianity as a whole. The Holy Spirit is the dinosaur's *mahout*. The guidance of the Holy Spirit allows for genuine development and prevents the dinosaur from losing its way.

> Paul's interest is not in the Jesus-tradition, but in Christ as the one who brings the new being and the New Age. In his death and resurrection the old powers are overthrown, and new possibilities of life open up for those who believe in him and are in him. This was not just one more divine initiative, but the definitive and final one, final in the sense that everything that follows is its outworking. Nothing could ever be the same again, and it was Paul's enormous and unique task

to work out what this meant for the individual, the church, and the universe.[2]

In the years between the historical life of Jesus Christ and the conversion of another major contributor to the history of the church as dinosaur, the Emperor Constantine, the church focused primarily on survival. Christianity spent its first three centuries as an outlawed organisation, unable to possess property or make any great sociological impact. Early Christian meetings gathered in the houses of well-to-do individuals. After the ban was lifted by the Emperor, the church's private property grew quickly through donations from pious and wealthy people. The Lateran Palace was the first significant donation, given by Constantine himself. From the fourth century, this Palace of the Lateran on Piazza San Giovanni became the principal residence of the popes, for the next thousand years.

However, the idea of a 'pope' did not exist from the beginning. Although, from the beginning, there were prominent church leaders whose authority was recognised, mostly because they were people who had known the apostles personally, there was no central authority in the church as such. It was not until several centuries after Christ's death that the church began to develop into the 'Roman Catholic Church,' as we think of it today. This fact allows non-Catholics to see such later developments as a corruption of the original message of Christianity, however, for those who recognise the inevitability of the dinosaur syndrome, such historical development is not only inevitable but also mysteriously guided, although this does not guarantee every eventuality, as the Holy Spirit never interferes with human free will.

Constantine's Edict of Milan legalised Christianity in 313, and later, his declaration of Christianity as the state religion of the Empire in 380 changed both the status and the style of the Christian church. The Edict had authority and effect throughout East and West as it was issued in the names of both the Emperor Constantine, who ruled the West, and Licinius, who ruled the East. They had come together in Milan for the wedding of

2. John Ziesler, *Pauline Christianity*, Revised Edition, Oxford, 1990, pp 145-9

Constantine's younger half-sister with Licinius. Such very human bonds allow the Holy Spirit to effect otherwise impossible liaisons. But it was the actual conversion of Constantine himself in 318AD that resulted in the church adopting a governmental structure which mirrored that of the Roman Empire. As in the Roman Empire itself, geographical provinces were ruled by governors (these were called bishops in the imitative template adopted by the church) based in the major city of each. (ἐπίσκο–ποι *episkopoi* means 'overseer' in Greek.) Soon, bishops of such major cities in the empire as Jerusalem, Alexandria, Antioch, Rome, and Constantinople, emerged as pre-eminent. It was natural that Rome would eventually become the most important of these. Not only was it the capital of the empire, but it was the city where the apostles Peter and Paul had been martyred. Some would see this connection between the Roman Empire and the church as providential; others would see it as betrayal of the original message of Jesus Christ. Roman Catholicism in its identification of itself as 'apostolic' (one of the four marks of the church as 'one, holy, catholic and apostolic') traces its history back to the original apostles, especially the apostle Peter, who is considered to have been the first pope. Every pope since then is regarded as his spiritual successor. Pope Benedict XVI, the present pope, is, for instance, the 265th pope after St Peter.

After the end of the Roman Empire, the term *Curia* was used to designate the administrative apparatus of the Roman Catholic Church. It provides the central organisation for the correct functioning of the church and the achievement of its mission. *Curia* in medieval Latin meant court, in the sense of 'royal court' rather than 'court of law'. The Roman Curia can be loosely compared to cabinets in Western forms of governance. Each of thirteen Congregations is led by a prefect, who is a cardinal.

The Roman Bishop Leo I (440-461) is considered by historians to have been the first pope to have claimed ultimate authority over all Christendom. In his writings one can find all the traditional arguments for papal authority. 'Thou art Peter and upon this rock I will build my church' writ large. Leo's claims were strengthened by his own impressive career as Bishop of Rome. In 445 he received the express support of the Emperor Valentian, who declared that the Bishop of Rome should be law for all. In 451, Leo called the important Council of Chalcedon, which put to rest christological issues that had been plaguing the church. In other words, he organised the definition of the person who had founded the church in the first place, in a way that would become normative for Roman Catholics from then on. In 452, he impressively saved Rome from Attila the Hun. When Leo met the warrior at the gates of Rome to persuade him to spare the city, Attila, according to legend, saw Peter and Paul marching with the pope to defend their city. In 455 Leo was not as successful with Vandal invaders. He led negotiations with them preventing the burning of Rome but he could not stop its being plundered.

Human, all-too-human, willfulness on both sides certainly contributed to the so-called 'East-West Schism' of 1054, which split Christianity into two major divides almost immediately after it celebrated its first millennium. Roman legates travelled to Constantinople to force the Patriarch Cerularius to recognise the church of Rome's claim to be head and mother of the other churches. Cerularius refused. So, the leader of the Latin embassy, Cardinal Humbert, hardly remembered for his diplomacy, rode his horse on 16 July 1054, into the Cathedral of the Hagia Sophia in Constantinople, during the celebration of the liturgy, to lay a Bull of excommunication on the high altar, despite the fact that the reigning pope had died in the meantime. Cerularius was understandably enraged by this offensive gesture and in turn excommunicated Cardinal Humbert and the other legates accompanying him. This series of unfortunate circumstances sparked off the so-called 'Great Schism' of Christendom. After it, the churches remaining in communion with the See of Rome, (the diocese of Rome and its bishop, the pope, as first patriarch) have been known as 'Catholic', while the Eastern churches that rejected the pope's authority have generally been known as 'Orthodox' or 'Eastern Orthodox'. Is it consoling to note that in 1965, almost a thousand years later – how slowly these dinosaurs move – the Pope and the Patriarch of Constantinople nullified these anathemas of 1054 in gestures of good will towards one another.

* * *

For nearly its first 1000 years, therefore, the Catholic Church presided over the total life of Christendom and animated its laws, customs, literature, art, and architecture. If you were a Christian in Europe, you belonged to the Catholic Church. Any Christianity other than the Catholic Church was a heresy, not a denomination. And this also means that for the first thousand years of Christianity there was no 'Roman Catholicism' as we know it today, simply because our present understanding of it is coloured by its opposition to rivals who did not then exist as such. At that time, there was no Orthodoxy or Protestantism from which to distinguish Roman Catholicism. There was only, with a very few exceptions, the 'one, holy, catholic and apostolic church' affirmed by the early creeds. This was the body of Christian believers all over the world, united by common traditions, beliefs, church structure and worship. If we had been as careful about the first of these so-called 'hallmarks' of the Church as we have been about the last, we might have done more to preserve the unity which is such an essential feature of Christianity, echoing Christ's insistent plea to the Father: 'that they may all be one. As you, Father, are in me and I am in you, may they also be in us, so that the world may believe that you have sent me.'[3]

> Institutional religion, and certainly Christianity the religion, is always a human construct. It is itself a work of human hands and manned [sic] by ordinary men and women who are no more gifted by the grace of God than the rest of us ... Christians must recognise the fact that they have regularly distorted the truth of the faith of Jesus, in various ways and to varying degrees over virtually the whole history of their religion.[4]

Even after the Great Schism, the Roman Catholic Church continued to dominate Europe throughout the Middle Ages and popes were powerful monarchs, epitomised by Pope Innocent III (1160-1216). He was a member of a famous Italian family, the Contis, who produced no less than nine popes. Innocent took the Muslim capture of Jerusalem in 1187 as a sign of divine judgement against the corruption of the church, and so set about

---

3. John 17:21
4. James P. Mackey, *Christianity and Creation, The Essence of the Christian Faith and its Future among Religions, A Systematic Theology*, Continuum, New York & London, 2006, pp 397

ring fencing what he called 'the liberty of the church' from the self-serving interests of secular princes. He wished to establish the autonomy of the church, for very good reasons. Local princes and foreign powers were interfering in church government and heavily involved in the selection of bishops. The church should be autonomous and capable of defending herself, Innocent believed. Joseph Stalin famously asked an adviser, dismissively, 'How many divisions does the pope have?' implying that without divisions any leader is powerless. Innocent III would have shared this view. Autonomy, for him, required that the church should have its own '*patrimonium*' controlled by the papacy. This translated itself practically into territorial claims.

Innocent shored up and consolidated that section of central Italy which was regarded as belonging to the church. These became known as 'the Papal States'. As pope, he became one of the leading jurists of his time and put himself in control of a vast and comprehensive ecclesiastical machinery which regulated in minute detail the moral and social behaviour of the whole medieval Christian world dominated by Roman Catholicism. During his reign he influenced the succession of the Holy Roman Empire, excommunicated King John of England, annulled *Magna Carta*, mediated disputes between France and England, and launched a crusade in the East, as well as the Albigensian crusade into France. The success of his endeavours created as many problems as it solved. The church became more like *Tyrannosaurus Rex*, the dinosaur of whom we have been able to reconstruct the skeletons of some thirty specimens around the world. 'Stan,' as specimen BHI 3033 in the Manchester Museum is affectionately called, was a bipedal carnivore with a massive skull balanced by a long, heavy tail. The church became, more and more, a skeleton built in this image. The first Inquisition for the suppression of heresy, for instance, was established in Languedoc in 1184.

Continuing the story of the Roman Catholic dinosaur, popes and emperors squabbled over a variety of issues, and German rulers, in particular, routinely treated the Papal States as part of their own realm on whichever occasion they chose to muscle their way into Italy. As early as 781, Charlemagne had codified the regions over which the pope would be temporal sovereign.

It was always understood that such property belonged to the pope's 'temporal' power as opposed to his 'spiritual' power. So, at all times, the church itself was conscious of its dinosaur dimension in contrast to its inner spiritual reality. The somewhat ambiguous cooperation between the papacy and the Carolingian dynasty climaxed in 800, when Pope Leo III crowned Charlemagne as the first 'Emperor of the Romans' (*Augustus Romanorum*). The precise nature of the relationship between popes and emperors – and between the Papal States and the Empire – was never very clear. Was the pope a sovereign ruler of a separate realm in central Italy, or were the Papal States just a part of the Frankish Empire over which the pope had administrative control? Or were the Holy Roman Emperors vicars of the pope (as a sort of Arch-emperor) ruling Christendom, with the pope directly responsible only for the environs of Rome? Such questions floated ambiguously without receiving satisfactory answers.

The Papal States, those territories under direct sovereign rule of the pope, covered most of the modern Italian regions of Romagna, Marche, Umbria and Lazio. By 1300, these Papal States, along with the rest of the Italian principalities, were effectively independent, they were disengaged from predatory surrounding rulers. The 1357 *Constitutiones Egidiane* mark a watershed in their legal history. These were six books of law which formed the first historic constitution of the Papal States, and the highest law in central Italy, which remained in effect until 1816.

Another important acquisition for the Papal States was Avignon in France. Following a period of strife between Pope Boniface VIII and King Philip IV of France, the French were determined to improve their situation. When the pope died and his successor also died eight months later, a deadlocked conclave finally elected a Frenchman as pope in 1305. Clement V, realising the fraught relationships he was inheriting, declined to move to Rome, and remained in France, moving his whole court, in 1309, to Avignon, where it remained for the next 68 years. During this period the city of Avignon itself was added to the Papal States; it remained a papal possession even after the popes returned to Rome. It was later seized and incorporated into France during the French Revolution. But from 1305 to 1378, the popes lived in this papal enclave of Avignon, and were under the influence of the French kings in what became known by the rest of the church as the 'Babylonian Captivity'.

During the Renaissance, papal territories expanded greatly, notably under Popes Alexander VI and Julius II. Alexander became a byword for papal depravity. However, so accustomed were the people of Rome to corruption in high places that they apparently only once publicly jeered this pope as he arrived at the gates of the city, not because he was there to await his mistress, but because he was wearing a silly hat unworthy of a supreme pontiff.

After the death of Innocent VIII on 25 July 1492, Roderic de Borgia was elected on 11 August 1492. He took the name Alexander. While there was never substantive proof of bribery, the rumour was that Borgia, with his great wealth, had succeeded in buying the largest number of votes at the conclave. The later Pope Leo X strongly criticised the election and the winning candidate saying: 'Now we are in the power of a wolf, the most rapacious perhaps that this world has ever seen. And if we do not flee, he will inevitably devour us all.' At first, Alexander's reign was as orderly as it was splendiferous. Soon his nepotism, his passion for endowing his relatives at the church's expense, took over. He had four, and possibly five, children by his long time mistress. He made one of his sons, Cesar, while a seventeen-year-old student at Pisa, Archbishop of Valencia.

The corrupt state of the papacy and the Curia, which had been peopled by Alexander's family and cronies, led to a number of prophetic heralds of the later Reformation. One such was the John the Baptist figure of Savonarola, the ascetic Dominican, who appealed for a general council to confront church scandals. He launched intemperate attacks against curial and papal corruption. He certainly had never learnt to dance with the dinosaur. Alexander VI excommunicated him, of course, but as he was unable to get him into his own hands, he browbeat the Florentine government into condemning the reformer to death. He was burnt at the stake on 23 May 1498.

Two popes who were probably most influential in their support for the fruitful cross-fertilisation between the church and the great artists of the Italian Renaissance, were Julius II (Pope from November 1503 to February 1513) and Leo X (March 1513-December 1521). Julius was elected when his predecessor, Pius III, resigned 26 days after his elevation. He was elected with the help of lavish promises and bribes at a conclave lasting a single day. Forceful, ruthless and violent, he set out to extend the Papal States. He led a military campaign, himself in full armour at its head, returning Perugia and Bologna to his jurisdiction. Historians score him high for military prowess but low for spiritual integrity. He was self-willed, easily angered and sensual. As cardinal he fathered three children and was called by his people *'Il terribile'*. However, on his death he was hailed by Italians as one who freed their country from foreign domination.

Pope Julius II laid the foundation stone for the new St Peter's and arranged for the cost to be defrayed by the sale of indulgences. His successor, Leo X, a polished renaissance prince and a masterly politician, was recklessly extravagant and sold ecclesiastical offices and even cardinal's hats to finance his projects. To pay for the huge expense of the basilica of St Peter which he had inherited from his predecessor, he renewed the indulgences authorised by Julius and arranged for these to be promoted by preachers throughout Christendom. In January 1517 the notorious John Tetzel began preaching in Germany. Is it any wonder that the iconoclasm of Martin Luther (1483-1546) began to take effect?

During these unsavoury times the pope became one of Italy's most important secular rulers as well as being head of the church. He became involved in fighting wars and in signing treaties with other sovereigns. Hegemony was always contested and it took until the 16th century for the pope to have any genuine control over all his territories.

Following the Reformation, another failure in human relations and basic diplomacy, also in the 16th century, the church 'in communion with the Bishop of Rome' used the term 'Catholic' to distinguish itself from the various Protestant churches that split off. The Reformation had begun as an attempt to reform the church by devout members who opposed what they perceived to be corruption, false doctrines, and ecclesiastical malpractice – especially the teaching and the sale of indulgences and the selling and buying of clerical offices. However, the movement turned into a revolution and many protesting groups left the church and set up their own denominations which they believed to be truer manifestations of the original spirit of Christ's teaching and example.

The reaction within the Roman Catholic Church was to initiate a counter-reformation. As well as being an attempt to deal with the obvious corruption which the Protestant reformers had pointed out so strikingly, it was also an attempt to redefine the Roman Catholic Church. The Council of Trent tried to achieve this goal in contradistinction to the Protestant churches who had now set themselves up in opposition.

Most of the territories regarded as Papal States were eventually absorbed into the Kingdom of Italy by 1860. The final portion, the city of Rome, was appropriated ten years later, in 1870 and was declared capital city of Italy in March 1861 by the first Italian parliament which met in the kingdom's old capital Turin. However, they could not take possession of their capital because Napoleon III kept a French garrison there protecting Pope Pius IX. The Italian opportunity came when the Franco-Prussian War broke out in July 1870. Napoleon III had to recall his garrison from Rome. Following the collapse of the Second French Empire at the battle of Sedan, it became impossible for him ever again to send an imperial French garrison back to Rome. Widespread public demonstrations took place over all of Italy demanding that the Italian government take back their capital city. King Victor Emmanuel II sent Count Gustavo Ponza di San Martino to Pius IX with a personal letter offering a face-saving proposal to allow the peaceful entry of the Italian army into Rome, under the guise of offering protection to the pope. The Papal States were then reduced to Latium, in the immediate hinterland of Rome.

In a later attempt to compensate for the loss, and provide some geographical base for the Roman Catholic Church, the Lateran Treaty of 1929 brought the Vatican city-state into existence. These Lateran Agreements were incorporated into the Constitution of the Italian Republic in 1947. The treaty spoke of the Vatican as a new creation, and not as the remnant of the former Papal States which had extended throughout most of central Italy from 756 to 1870. Vatican City was thus a compromise and a sop to allow the Holy See the political benefits of territorial sovereignty. The treaty was signed by the Cardinal Secretary of State, Pietro Gasparri, on behalf of the Holy See, and by Prime Minister Benito Mussolini on behalf of the Kingdom of Italy on 7 June 1929. The golden pen used for the signing, later presented to *Il Duce*, was supplied by Pope Pius XI himself. And so the Vatican as we understand this term today was born less than a hundred years ago.

This Vatican City, officially *Stato della Città del Vaticano*, 'State of the City of the Vatican,' is a landlocked sovereign city-state within the city of Rome itself. It has approximately 44 hectares (110 acres) and a population of about 800. The territory includes St Peter's Square, marked off from the territory of Italy by a simple white line. St Peter's Square itself is reached through the Via della Conciliazione which runs from the Tiber River to the basilica. This grand approach was constructed by Mussolini in something of a conciliatory gesture after the conclusion of the Lateran Treaty. The name 'Vatican' predates Christianity and is the name of the mountain (*Mons Vaticanus*) of which Vatican City forms a part. The former 'Vatican Fields' beside this mountain are where St Peter's Basilica, the Apostolic Palace, the Sistine Chapel and various museums were put, along with other buildings.

* * *

The Second Vatican Council (1962-65) was perhaps the biggest meeting in the history of the world.[5] A gathering of over 2,000 Catholic priests, bishops, and cardinals from all over the world met in Rome four autumns in a row, eight weeks at a time. Their average age was 60. These most influential practitioners of Catholicism debated the very nature of their faith. Between the opening and closing dates, 11 October 1962 to 8 December 1965, 253 of them died and 296 were added. Between deaths, depart-

---

5. John W. O'Malley, *What Happened at Vatican II*, The Belknap Press of Harvard University Press, Cambridge, Massachusetts, 2008. I rely heavily on this excellent summary of a comparatively recent and complex event. For the remainder of this section I shall refer to this work with the page number in a square bracket.

ures and new arrivals, it is estimated that a total of 2,860 attended part or all of the four periods. Between *periti* (the name given to those expert theologians who came to advise the bishops), journalists, observers, and guests, there were always at least 7,500 people present in Rome at any given time because of Vatican II.

116 different countries were represented: 36% of these came from Europe; 34% represented the Americas; 20% came from Asia and Oceania; 10% were from Africa. This is in contrast to previous councils. Only 750 bishops participated in Vatican I, and at the Council of Trent, the least well attended of all the councils, only twenty-nine bishops attended the opening. Even at the largest sessions of the famous Tridentine Council, the number of voting members rarely exceeded 200.

Vatican II was the twenty-first ecumenical council in the church's history. By 'ecumenical' is meant church-wide and not just local. The first such ecumenical council was held in Nicea in 325. This was thirteen years after the conversion of the emperor Constantine. The first seven ecumenical councils, until the Second Council of Nicea in 728, involved most of the Christian community. After that, the so-called 'ecumenical' councils were restricted to the Roman Catholic Church so that other Christians would question their right to be called ecumenical in the first place. How could one particular branch of Christianity decide on such important issues as papal infallibility, for instance, without general consensus from the whole Christian community? Many Christians seek to return to the teachings of these seven councils when the church was undivided and to start again from there. Others have a very mystical interpretation of the first seven councils, mirroring the seven days of creation. They hold that the eighth ecumenical council, representing the eighth day and the perfection of Christian communion, can only take place in a perfectly united Christendom on the last day in the New Jerusalem.

Roman Catholics have a less mystical and more incarnational view. The whole church assembled in council is a most potent instrument of the Holy Spirit who has promised to guide the lumbering dinosaur until the end of time. And so for the Roman Catholic Church the ecumenical council which was Vatican II must be seen as one of the most important meetings ever held.

People even referred to it as 'the end of the Constantinian era', an allusion to the fourth century situation already described whereby official recognition and privileged status was granted to the church by the Roman Emperor Constantine. In other words, Vatican II had ended a sixteen-hundred-year-old paradigm of the Roman Catholic Church in its imperial and colonial guise. Others called it 'the end of the Counter Reformation', which referred to that image of the church as an embattled and conservative *ancien régime* which defined itself by opposition and contradistinction to the many headed hydra of Protestantism.

To understand the context of this monster meeting we have to situate it in what has been termed the Catholic Church's 'long nineteenth century'. This contentious period, as far as Catholicism was concerned, dated from the French Revolution to the end of the pontificate of Pius XII in 1958. We have to see it in terms of the rise of socialism and communism in the first half of the twentieth century, and the traumatic experiences of the world which began with World War II, less than two decades before the council. Finally and more immediately still, there was the Cold War and the Cuban Missile Crisis which threatened the planet with nuclear annihilation. It was as if the world anticipated another extinction event similar to the one which had obliterated the dinosaurs.

And as soon as the meeting began the battle was joined between two warring parties: 'Nobody expected that almost as soon as the council opened two groups of leaders, both relatively small, would emerge from among those thousands of bishops, and that the rest of the bishops would have to judge between the two sides not only on a number of specific issues but also on a general orientation of the council' [290].

There were three overarching concerns dominating the discussions. First: How the church would deal with change. Here they were caught between two imperatives: if they adulterated, altered or withheld anything of the original message of Jesus Christ, the church would lose its soul, its very reason for existence. And yet, on the other hand, the church would have to recognise that the message of Jesus Christ is not an abstraction above and beyond the human beings who first received it, or the human beings who have interpreted and passed it on through the centuries. The message entered the historical process, and by so doing it must, to some extent, become subject to change. By definition a transcendent message, it also by definition is meant for men and women of all times and cultures and so must be made meaningful for them [299].

The two camps fell on either side of this important divide. The conservatives defended aggressively the 'no change' policy. The progressives were influenced by new philosophies of history and theories of the development of doctrine throughout history. Words like *Aggiornamento*, and *ressourcement* became the catch cries of the second group, synonyms for change and in the ears of the conservatives, euphemisms for renaissance. Many were in favour of 'return to the sources,' dumping all the accretions which had gathered like barnacles on the side of the ship in between. So the battle was fought in depth and in detail and, as a result, the final text which was voted by the council as a whole was always a compromise between the two points of view.

The second area which became significant was what became known as 'collegiality.' This was essentially a question of the relationship which should pertain between bishops, or the episcopal hierarchy, and the pope. 'What kind of authority did the bishops have over the church at large when they acted collectively, that is, collegially; how was that authority exercised in relationship to the pope; and how was collegiality different from 'Conciliarism' (supremacy of a council over the pope), a position condemned in the fifteenth century and repeatedly condemned thereafter? [7] Collegiality became the lightning-rod issue of the council [163]. It galvanised the centripetal tendencies into full collision with the centrifugal. The first group condemned it as 'unworkable, unacceptable, dangerous, even heretical'. Conciliarism and Gallicanism had both been condemned by popes. Conservatives put collegiality into these same categories and regarded it as incompatible with papal primacy. The progressive group on the other hand regarded collegiality as the linchpin of the centre-periphery relationship [311]. Bishops, they said, are not branch managers of local offices of the Holy See [304].

The third underlying issue concerned the style with which the church should communicate and operate? How does it present itself, how does it 'do business'? – such a 'style' choice is an identity choice, a personality choice. Could that be a style less autocratic and more collaborative [307], one that eschews secret oaths, anonymous denunciations, and inquisitorial tactics? [308] In fact, the documents issuing from the council were already expressive of such a shift. There was a marked substitution of a rhetorical form for the judicial and legislative forms that had characterised previous councils [306] – canons, anathemas, verdicts of guilty-as-charged found no place. The Roman Synod of 1960, the 'dress rehearsal' for Vatican II, issued 755 canons. The council, which ended five years later, issued not a single one. 'On the final outcome of the council the minority left more than a set of finger-prints, which means that it left its mark on the three issues-under-the-issues. On the centre-periphery issue the minority never really lost control. It was in that regard so successful that with the aid of Paul VI the centre not only held firm and steady but, as the decades subsequent to the council have irrefutably demonstrated, emerged even stronger. From the outset the contest was unequal. The council was held in the centre, named for the centre, operated to a large extent with the equipment of the centre, and was destined to be interpreted and implemented by the centre. The creation of the Synod of Bishops severed collegiality, the doctrine empowering the periphery, from institutional grounding … Collegiality, the linchpin in the centre-periphery relationship promoted by the majority, ended up an abstract teaching without point of entry into the social reality of the church. It ended up an ideal, no match for the deeply entrenched system' [311].

But there were some advances made by this council. Roman Catholics had been forbidden to take part in dialogue with other Christians until they were encouraged by Vatican II to engage with people of different denominations, other religions, or none at all. 'Such dialogue,' *Gaudium et Spes* [#92] assured us, 'excludes no one.'

Just as St John appropriated the Greek word *logos* and used it to describe a miraculous reality never before envisaged or contemplated in the history of the universe, so too Pope John XXIII inserted into the vocabulary of the Roman Catholic Church the word 'dialogue', which takes on a refurbished and mysterious meaning in its new surroundings and context. For these last fifty years after Vatican II, the Roman Catholic Church has moved from an idiom of anathema to an idiom of dialogue. Instead of shunning and condemning heretics, pagans, infidels and schismatics, Catholics have been taught to refer instead to 'separated' brothers and sisters.[6]

We are 'unfinished' animals who complete ourselves through culture. There is a difference between the evolutionary process which unfolded the animal, vegetable and mineral world and the future evolution of the planet, since humanity established itself and became the dominant species. Animals are determined by nature. They do nothing more than instinctively fulfil the pattern inscribed in their genes and chromosomes. They are DNA docile. Our DNA provides us also with a Lego set to build our own completion. Ours is not a blueprint encoded in our genes, it is the basic score for an unfinished symphony. The future of the planet now depends upon us. Our decisions, the way in which we propose to develop ourselves, the direction we take – all these will determine the future for us all. We complete or finish ourselves through culture. We are what Cifford Geertz has called 'cultural artefacts'. We become who we are 'under the guidance of cultural patterns, historically created systems of meaning in terms of which we give form, order, point and direction to our lives.' Religion is always one such cultural artefact. The forces of nature want to grow a roof over our heads where none was intended. We are naturally inclined to build elaborate nests, immoveable dams, honeycombed hives and subterranean anthills. Our automatic response to complexity and danger is to construct an indestructible labyrinth around our deepest, most vulnerable and fragile self. We are all aware of this force of gravity in ourselves, the compelling drive towards universal compendiums and ungainsayable creeds. We long for the harmonious luxury of certitude expressed in 'the geometrical absolutisms of an orthodoxy.'

Surely we have to win back for Christianity the purity and originality which is embodied in the person of Jesus Christ. And the way to get to that original meaning, the founding Spirit, the paradigmatic Person, could be by humble and truthful dialogue. Christianity, at its source and in its constitution, is not a set of

6. For a more extended treatment of this subject see *I Must Be Talking To Myself, Dialogue in the Roman Catholic Church*, Dublin, Veritas, 2004

propositions, a formula of any kind. It is not something which can be owned or controlled by anyone or any group. The church is a relationship between persons. It is founded on a person, by a person, through other particular persons. What the church is, its reality, is handed on, handed down, from persons to persons in a relationship of faith, hope and love. Our dialogue between Christians is not about a written text, it is about a living reality. We have no mandate to focus all our critical faculties on words or formulae which come down to us as more or less adequate encapsulations of the truth which is incarnate in the person of Jesus Christ. All such written texts are secondary theology in comparison with the primary theology which is unwritten and requires spiritual transmission from person to person because it is an essentially inexpressible mystery. All our formulae are paradigms of a deeper reality which Christians who have preceded us have tried to express by the inspiring power of the Holy Spirit. Our dialogue, which necessarily involves study of such dogmatic formulae, cannot focus exclusively on these texts, it must concentrate also upon the reality, the Person, the relationship which seeks expression therein.

The word 'dogma' in Greek means 'that which seems right.' The word 'heresy' comes from the Greek word meaning to select, to section yourself off from the fullness of truth. No Christian wants to do this. That is why it is imperative for all Christians to enter into dialogue about the full meaning of the mystery in which we all believe, and which it is our privilege to find enunciated in many and various ways throughout the 2000 year history of this tradition. Unity is an essential mark of the church founded by Christ: that they may be one, his constant prayer. As disciples of Christ in dialogue we cannot afford to situate ourselves exclusively in front of any text, any written words. We have to situate ourselves together in the space between those formulae and the living persons who are the authors, the objects and the only purpose of any such creedal expressions. Our dialogue is in and through the Holy Spirit. And as Karl Rahner puts it: 'In the Spirit of God all of us "know" something more simple, more true and more real than we can know or express at the level of our theological concepts.'[7]

7. Karl Rahner, *Theological Investigations* 14, p 251

History has taught us, with heart-rending examples, that the language instinct in each one of us is primary. In the infamous Atlantic slave trade on the tobacco, cotton, coffee and sugar plantations, greedy landowners would put to work slaves of different ethnicities to get more work and less talk out of them. 'When speakers of different languages have to communicate to carry out practical tasks ... they develop a make-shift jargon called a pidgin.'[8] These are sometimes haphazard strings of words borrowed from the language of the colonisers or plant-ation owners. In certain places this 'Pidgin' can become a *lingua franca*. Dialogue is showing, pointing towards, sharing the things which we surmise, rather than the creeds which we have formulated. Our dialogue should be about the reality which we have inherited rather than about the 'pidgin' which we have in-vented to express it. If I want to make myself understood by someone who has no common language with me, I take them to the sea and I point at it and say 'sea' several times. I then gesture to them to tell me their word for this reality. They then repeat their word and we have understood each other although we have different, incomprehensible words for the same reality. How true this is of all that we 'know' about Christianity, about the incarnation, about the resurrection, about the Trinity, about the Eucharist. These are words that we use to express a mystery, a reality beyond our grasp. When each of us describes the words we use, and the explanations which we give to these words, then we shall know so much more about the unknowable mystery.

The church of Christ is founded on a silent personal mystery which can never be translated adequately into human words. All speech about this reality is necessarily fumbling: a stab at the truth. Tradition (handing on) of the mystery always risks be-trayal. And yet we have to formulate the *mirabilia dei* into some enduring shape so that it is never forgotten and so that it can be passed on from generation to generation. However, like the written notation which preserves great musical works, the en-codement is nothing without the music which must be realised in every generation. Unless the music is actually heard it re-mains a disembodied skeleton in the score. Similarly, all creedal

8. Steven Pinker, *The Language Instinct*, Penguin Books, 1994, p 32ff

formulae, dogmatic tracts, articles of faith, articulations of the mysteries of Christianity, are humble servants of a much greater and quite other reality which no person in the world can claim as a possession. No person or people, no church or catechism, no dogma or denomination incorporates the mystery of our faith. Definitive incorporation of this mystery took place in the person of Jesus Christ. Post-Christian elaboration of this must be the work of the Holy Spirit.

Vatican Council I (1869-1870) cast a very long shadow. No aspect of the nineteenth century was more important for the Catholic Church than the new prominence which was given to the papacy because of that council's definition of papal infallibility. By this Vatican definition, the doctrine of the pope's infallibility become *de fide*, that is, a truth necessary to be believed, as being included in the original divine revelation and, if you are a Roman Catholic you cannot not believe it. So this dogmatic pronouncement needs very careful clarification.

Infallibility is the dogma in Roman Catholic theology which ensures the progress of the dinosaur along the right path. However corrupt or contaminated it may seem to be, there is an in-built guarantee of the presence of Christ with his church until the end of time. Practically speaking, this boils down to the promise that, because of the action of the Holy Spirit, the pope is preserved from error when he solemnly declares or promulgates to the universal church a dogmatic teaching on faith or morals. This implies that the particular dogma is contained in divine revelation, or at least is intimately connected to divine revelation.

Papal infallibility is one of the channels of the infallibility of the whole church (or, more properly, the indefectibility of the whole church). Once again, this is based on Christ's promise to be with his church until the end of time and the belief that the Holy Spirit will not allow the church to err in its belief or teaching under certain circumstances. The church is infallible in all her members, laity as well as hierarchy. The Word of God as given by Christ to the apostles was possessed by the whole church and meant to be studied, meditated, and handed on by all. The bishops, by their particular title, were the judges of the faith, but by no means the guardians in an absolute sense.

In fact, in Roman Catholic tradition, the *sensus fidelium* or the 'sense of the faithful,' is the idea that the belief of good and honest Catholics is one of the valid sources of truth in Catholic theology. This is something which religious leaders are supposed to consult when making decisions about Catholic doctrine. The *sensus fidelium* was one way of discovering the tradition of the church. This tradition manifests itself in various ways at various times: 'Sometimes by the mouth of the episcopacy, sometimes by the doctors, sometimes by the people, sometimes by liturgies, rites, ceremonies, and customs, by events, disputes, movements, and all those other phenomena which are comprised under the name of history.'[9] These words were written by John Henry Newman five years after the dogma of the Immaculate Conception had been proclaimed and ten years before the definition of papal infallibility. Newman, who was beatified on 19 December 2010, by Pope Benedict XVI, became a convert to Roman Catholicism in 1845. Originally, he had been an evangelical Oxford clergyman in the Church of England. Less than two months after the beginning of the First Vatican Council (8 December 1869), Newman wrote to his Ordinary of Birmingham, Bishop William B. Ullathorne, expressing his opposition to defining papal infallibility as a dogma of faith and describing it as a 'great calamity,' believing that the time was 'inopportune'. On 23 July 1870 Newman saw the definition of papal infallibility which had been passed five days earlier by Vatican Council I. He was 'pleased at its moderation'; the 'terms used' were 'vague and comprehensive', and he personally had no difficulty in accepting it. He was sure that divine intervention had prevented the extreme ultramontanes, including the pope, from getting through a much stronger definition. He feared that the religious devotion of the hierarchy of his day to a certain type of obedience and doctrinal uniformity could have the effect of allowing the notion of the *consensus fidelium* to recede into the background.

Newman ended the article with an excerpt from Fr Dalgairn's account of the Council of Ephesus. The description of the faithful joyously escorting the bishops home with torches at

---

9. John Henry Newman, 'On Consulting the Faithful', *The Rambler*, July, 1859

the end of the day he took as an image of the ideal situation in the church. 'I think certainly that the *Ecclesia docens* is more happy when she has such enthusiastic partisans about her as are here represented, than when she cuts off the faithful from the study of her divine doctrines and the sympathy of her divine contemplations, and requires from them a *fides implicita* in her word, which in the educated classes will terminate in indifference, and in the poorer in superstition.'[10]

Originally when a non-Italian pope was elected, he was said to be *papa ultramontano*, a pope from beyond the mountains (meaning the Alps). Foreign students at medieval Italian universities were also referred to as ultramontanes. The word was revived but the meaning reversed after the Protestant Reformation in France, to indicate the 'man beyond the mountains' located in Italy. In France, the name *ultramontain* was applied to people who supported papal authority in French political affairs, as opposed to the Gallican leanings of the indigenous French Catholic Church. From the 17th century, ultramontanism became closely associated with the Jesuits, who defended the superiority of popes over councils and kings, even in temporal questions. Within the Roman Catholic Church, ultramontanism was seen to have achieved a victory over conciliarism at the First Vatican Council with the pronouncement of papal infallibility. Other Christians not in full communion with Rome declared this as the triumph of what they termed 'the heresy of ultramontanism.' This term 'ultramontanism' had come to mean a religious philosophy that places strong emphasis on the prerogatives and powers of the pope. In particular, it asserts the superiority of papal authority over the authority of local temporal or spiritual hierarchies (including the local bishop). When Gladstone accused the Roman Church of having 'equally repudiated modern thought and ancient history' by making this pronouncement of infallibility, Newman affirmed that he had always believed in the doctrine, and had only feared the deterrent effect of its definition on conversions on account of acknowledged historical difficulties.

---

10. Samuel D. Femiano, *Infallibility of the Laity, the Legacy of Newman*, New York, Herder and Herder, 1967, p 132

It has to be remembered that this definition of infallibility was promulgated at a council attended by 750 bishops, where, as always, there was division between conservatives and those more open to change. Such divisions occur at every council, at every meeting, where human beings are present. The first group understands the reality of the church in terms of certain constants contained in the scriptures and the Christian tradition. Divine revelation, they believe, has crystallised in supra-temporal expressions handed down to us in a deposit of faith, translated by the magisterium of the church into static norms which cannot be changed.

The second group understand the reality of the church as the incarnation of God's redemptive plan, the record of which is available in the scriptures and the Christian tradition. However, to understand these documents of the past, it is necessary to place them in the historical context in which they were created. No one of us and nothing that exists on earth can escape the brand marks of time. This second group also believes that the future is unforeseen territory which will require of every institution, including the church, negotiation, development and change. The agreed formulations of any and every council, therefore, are hammered out between these two opposing worldviews and are·nearly always some form of *via media* between the two. This also allows those coming after the council to give a minimalist or a maximalist interpretation of the text, according to the preferences of the interpreter.

An example of this is to be found in one sentence from the Constitution on the Church, *Lumen Gentium*, of Vatican Council II, which some theologians viewed as an abdication of the church's historic (and to them compulsory) identification of itself alone as God's church, and by others as the 'crowbar to the wall of exclusivism':

> The one mediator, Christ, established and ever sustains here on earth his holy church, the community of faith, hope and charity, as a visible organisation through which he communicates truth and grace to all men … This is the sole church of Christ which in the creed we profess to be one, holy, catholic and apostolic, which our Saviour, after his resurrection, en-

trusted to Peter's pastoral care (Jn 21:17), commissioning him and the other apostles to extend and rule it (cf Mt 28:18, etc), and which he raised up for all ages as 'the pillar and main-stay of the truth' (1 Tim 3:15). This church, constituted and organised as a society in the present world, subsists in the Catholic Church, which is governed by the successor of Peter and by the bishops in communion with him. Nevertheless, many elements of sanctification and of truth are found out-side its visible confines. Since these are gifts belonging to the church of Christ, they are forces impelling towards Catholic unity.[11]

It is the second last sentence in this paragraph which changes the tone of the church's self-understanding. The conservative lobby at the council wished to maintain the original draft of this text which said that 'This church, constituted and organised as a society in the present world, is the Catholic Church, which is governed by the successor of Peter and by the bishops in com-munion with him.' The majority of the fathers present at the council were unhappy with this longstanding identification. They wished to establish that there was more to the church of Christ than the Holy Roman Catholic Church as gathered to-gether here in council. The words 'subsists in' (*subsistit*) re-placed the word 'is' (*est*) in the original text. The explanation for this change was delivered to the assembly 'as an expression more harmonious with the affirmation of ecclesial elements which are elsewhere.'[12] Vague and ambiguous as this explan-ation for the change may be, it reworded the longstanding phrase, which stated that the church of Christ is (Latin *est*) the Catholic Church. *Lumen Gentium* does recognise that other

---

11. *Lumen Gentium* 8, Flannery, Austin, ed *Vatican Council II: Constit-utions, Decrees, Declarations*, Northport, NY: Costello Publishing Co, 1996.
12. Along with the proposed text was included an official explanation of the changes made since the last public session in Nov-Jan 1963/4. These *relationes* included the following official explanation of the change of *est* to *subsistit in*:
> Quaedam verba mutuantur: loco «*est*», l. 21, dicitur «*subsistit in*», ut expressio melius concordet cum affirmatione de elementis ecclesi-alibus quae alibi *adsunt*.

Christian ecclesial communities, even if not included in the church of Jesus Christ, have elements of sanctification and of truth. Such a compromise allows conservatives to claim that this phrase 'subsists in' is nothing more than a paraphrase of the word 'is;' whereas it also allows more progressive theologians to claim a huge step forward in the recognition of the validity of other churches. According to such theologians, to say that the church of Christ 'subsists in' the Catholic Church introduces a distinction between the church of Christ and the Catholic Church. Catholic teaching had traditionally, until then, stated unequivocally that 'the Mystical Body of Christ and the Roman Catholic Church are one and the same thing,' as Pope Pius XII expressed it in his 1950 encyclical *Humani generis*. This particular sentence from *Lumen Gentium* of Vatican II will always stand. It does not mean 'is' and it does not mean 'is not'. In between these two parameters are endless nuances of interpretation which can be discussed and, indeed, have been discussed, theologically. But the phrase itself which was voted upon by the council fathers will remain.[13] This is the Holy Spirit's way of dancing with the dinosaurs and allowing Catholic theologians to remain between the Scylla of stating that the church of Christ subsists in other churches as it does in the Catholic Church, and the Charybdis of claiming that the church of Christ is exhausted in the Catholic Church, a claim that would falsely interpret Vatican II's doctrine on the elements of the church and of church membership.

Leonardo Boff, in his book *Church, Charism and Power: Liberation Theology and the Institutional Church*, took this phrase to mean that the one church of Christ 'is able to subsist in other Christian churches.'[14] The Congregation for the Doctrine of the

13. The version presented to the Council Fathers was subject, in accord with the rules of the Council, to the *processus verbales* in which the Council was asked to approve or reject the text as proposed, two days later, on 17 September 1964. Of the 2189 Council Fathers present, 2114 voted *placet*, 11 *non placet*, 63 *placet iuxta modum*, 1 did not vote. In accordance with the rules of the Council, this vote approved Chapter I and made it the official text of the first chapter of *Lumen Gentium*.

14. Leonardo Boff: Church: *Charism and Power: Liberation theology and the Institutional Church*. trs John W. Diercksmeier: Crossroad, New York, 1985: orig. pub. 1982

Faith replied to this possibility making it quite clear that this interpretation was, in their view, not justified. In response to Boff's assertion the CDF issued a *Notification* which states that 'the Council chose the word *subsistit* specifically to clarify that the true church has only one 'subsistence,' while outside her visible boundaries there are only *elementa Ecclesiae* which – being elements of the same church – tend and lead to the Catholic Church.'[15]

Cardinal Schönborn, Archbishop of Vienna explains that this teaching is summed up in the refusal of two extremes. On the one hand, ecclesial relativism – all churches have the same value and are more or less successful prefigurations of the heavenly church. And on the other hand, the affirmation that there is only the Catholic Church and that the rest is not church. The documents of any council of the church are always sober and balanced, rejecting extreme options.[16]

But this means that they are open to interpretation and subject to many conflicting views. There are those who see *Lumen Gentium's subsistit in* as leading to error and accuse its designers of trying to widen the church of Jesus Christ to almost all Christian sects, and to all world religions.

On the other hand we have almost the opposite point of view expressed by a bishop of the Roman Catholic Church:

> Lest we do not highlight sufficiently this important fact Vatican II was an Ecumenical Council, i.e. a solemn exercise of the magisterium of the church, i.e. the college of bishops gathered together with the Bishop of Rome and exercising a teaching function for the whole church. In other words, its vision, its principles and the direction it gave are to be followed and implemented by all, from the pope to the peasant farmer in the fields of Honduras.
>
> Since Vatican II there has been no such similar exercise of

15. Congregation for the Doctrine of the Faith, *Notification on the book of Father Leonardo Boff: 'The Church: charism and power'*: AAS 77 (1985) 758-759. This passage of the *Notification*, although not formally quoted in the '*Responsum*', is found fully cited in the Declaration *Dominus Jesus*, in note 56 of n 16
16. 'Dechristianization, the *subsistit in*, and the *motu proprio* according to Cardinal Schonborn', DICI, Monday 28 February 2011

teaching authority by the magisterium. Instead, a series of decrees, pronouncements and decisions which have been given various 'labels' stating, for example, that they must be firmly held to with 'internal assent' by the Catholic faithful, but in reality are simply the theological or pastoral interpretations or opinions of those who have power at the centre of the church. They have not been solemnly defined as belonging to the 'deposit of the faith' to be believed and followed, therefore, by all Catholics, as with other solemnly proclaimed dogmas.[17]

Bishop Dowling who worked for seventeen years with the Bishops' Conference Justice and Peace Department in South Africa, believes that 'we now have a leadership in the church … where one of the key Vatican II principles, collegiality in decision-making, is virtually non-existent.' He quotes the eminent emeritus Archbishop of Vienna, Cardinal Franz König, who wrote in 1999 – almost 35 years after Vatican II: 'In fact, however, *de facto* and not *de jure*, intentionally or unintentionally, the curial authorities working in conjunction with the pope have appropriated the tasks of the episcopal college. It is they who now carry out almost all of them.'[18]

Vatican Council I was a comparatively short council which had to be adjourned on 20 October 1870 because of the Franco-Prussian war (19 July 1870-10 May 1871). This war was the immediate occasion for the pope being stripped of most of the 'temporal power' at his disposal and later immured in the hastily established Vatican City State. In such circumstances, the emphasis of the First Vatican Council some weeks before, on the 'spiritual' power of the pope and his infallibility, is understandable. However, it should not be forgotten that 'infallibility' is the charism of the whole church and there are other manifestations of it than the very specific and, of course, crucial role of the pope.

Other channels described by Newman as being capable of

---

17. Taken from a lunchtime address given by Bishop Kevin Dowling CSsR to a group of leading laity in Cape Town, South Africa on 1 June 2010
18. 'My Vision of the Church of the Future', *The Tablet*, 27 March 1999, p 434

giving witness to the Church's tradition, all have a place in theological investigation. The teaching of the church regarding the infallibility of the faithful was never lost even though it had generally been ignored since the Council of Trent. Vatican II reasserted it saying that 'the entire body of the faithful ... cannot err in matters of belief. They manifest this special property ... when they show universal agreement in matters of faith and morals.'[18]

Pope Benedict XVI has said during an impromptu address to priests in Aosta in July 2005: 'The pope is not an oracle; he is infallible in very rare situations, as we know.' The infallible teachings of the pope must be based on, or at least not contradict, sacred tradition or sacred scripture, and they can only be infallible when he speaks *ex cathedra*. This Latin phrase meaning 'from the chair' is a technical term. The pope is not infallible in any of his words or teaching unless he explicitly intends to exercise such infallibility. The 'chair' referred to is not a literal one; it is a metaphor describing the pope's role, or his office, as the appointed teacher of Catholic doctrine: the chair was symbol of the teacher in the ancient world, and all bishops to this day have a *cathedra*, a seat or throne, as a symbol of their teaching and governing authority. The word cathedral comes from the place in which the 'chair' of the bishop in a diocese is placed. The pope is said to occupy the 'chair of Peter.'

In the sixth century, after the collapse of the Roman Empire, Benedict of Nursia combined the Roman genius for legislation with the Christian charism of *koinonia*, or life together in community, and wrote a Rule for monks which would help Christians to preserve the original community life described in *The Acts of the Apostles* and, at the same time, provide a sociological structure which would cope with the day-to-day struggle of human beings trying to live together in harmony. In this Rule the abbot of the community is described in great detail and with perceptive political acumen. One could say that he is Benedict's description of what the pope should be in the larger organisation of the universal church. In the microcosm of the monastery the abbot holds primacy over the others and is envisaged as more or less infallible in his eventual decisions, as far as those

19. *Lumen Gentium*, art 12

who are under his rule are concerned. However, such primacy and infallibility must be exercised with extreme care and in direct consultation with all the others in the community. In chapter 3 of the *Rule of Benedict*, 'Of Calling the Brethren to Council', it is clear that the principle of infallibility belongs to the community as a whole and that the abbot is simply the elected representative through whom this charism is exercised.

> Whenever any important business has to be done in the monastery, let the Abbot call together the whole community and state the matter to be acted upon.
>
> Then, having heard the brethren's advice, let him turn the matter over in his own mind and do what he shall judge to be most expedient.
>
> The reason we have said that all should be called for counsel is that the Lord often reveals to the younger what is best.

In a reunited Christendom many denominations would agree that the Bishop of Rome, the Pope, should have the first place. That seems to have been the pattern from the beginning in the ancient Christian world. Based on the antiquity of the protocol by which ecumenical councils have conceded some kind of universal primacy to the Bishops of Rome, participants in Anglican-Roman Catholic dialogues have acknowledged for decades that the pope would properly serve as the titular leader of a reunited church; the Anglicans, however, have in mind an honorary (non-jurisdictional) primacy such as the phrase *primus inter pares* implies. In one example of such acknowledgement, the International Anglican-Roman Catholic Commission for Unity and Mission, in its 2007 agreed statement *Growing Together in Unity and Mission*, 'urge[s] Anglicans and Roman Catholics to explore together how the ministry of the Bishop of Rome might be offered and received in order to assist our communions to grow towards full, ecclesial communion.' This would involve a specifically Christian concept of 'first' which would make the pope 'last' in terms of humility and service. *Primus inter pares*, meaning first among equals, is an ancient Latin phrase and a favourite of many Christian denominations, to describe a person who is the most senior of a group of people sharing the same rank or office. This is the pattern to which many Christians would return if the primacy of the pope were understood as a primacy of service or a primacy of love. Saint Ignatius of Antioch (50-117), one of the earliest bishop martyrs of the Christian church, addresses the Church of Rome as the church which presides in love. His phrase is often quoted by Anglican and Orthodox Christians as their preferred interpretation of such primacy. It appears to many outside the Catholic Church that this primacy of service, primacy of love, has been turned into a primacy of power and of jurisdiction. In a reunited Christendom, most Christians would be prepared to give the pope an all-embracing pastoral care but they would see the church on earth as essentially a conciliar church. Therefore, as in the *Rule of Benedict*, when problems arise, they should normally be solved through the meeting of a council, through a synod, which is seen as a continuation of the mystery of Pentecost. Christians would meet together, pray to the Holy Spirit and seek to reach a common mind. In the synod, the pope would have the first place but would be a member with other bishops. If the primacy of Peter, the primacy of the pope, is presented in strictly juridical terms then many insurmountable difficulties are raised, but if it is presented in a pastoral perspective, then there is a real possibility of meeting together because very widely in the Christian world today people can see the need for a certain primacy of pastoral initiative. The model is of Christ washing the feet of his disciples, Christ reminding us that 'the leaders of the Gentiles give orders to their servants but it shall not be so among you.' If that is our model, then there need not be a problem.[20]

20. Most of what I say here is taken from a dialogue with Bishop Kallistos Ware. Bishop Kallistos was born, Timothy Ware, in Bath, Somerset, in 1934 and was educated at Westminster School and Magdalen College, Oxford, where he took a Double First in Classics, as well as reading Theology. After joining the Orthodox Church in 1958, he travelled widely in Greece, staying in particular at the monastery of St John, Patmos, and he is familiar with the life of other Orthodox centres such as Mount Athos and Jerusalem. In 1966 he was ordained priest and became a monk, receiving the new name Kallistos. Since 1966 he has been back at Oxford as Spalding Lecturer in Eastern Orthodox Studies at the University. He also has pastoral charge of the Greek parish in Oxford. In 1970 he became a Fellow of Pembroke College,

We have to recognise, therefore, that the church is a twofold phenomenon. The esoteric church of St John (the 'heart' of the church), is distinct from the exoteric church of St Peter (the 'head' of the church). It was never the intention or the role of John to found a new church, that was always Peter's charism. St Augustine puts this in another way:[21]

> The church knows two lives which have been laid down and commended to her by God. One is through faith, the other through vision. The apostle Peter personifies the first life, John the second. The first has no place except on earth; it lasts only to the end of the present age and comes to an end in the next world. The second life has no end in the age to come, and its perfection is delayed until the end of the present age. And so Peter is told: 'Follow me,' while it is said of John: 'If it is my will that he remain until I come, what is that to you? You are to follow me.' To preserve the still and secret heart of the next life, John the Evangelist rested on Christ's breast: sublime knowledge proclaimed by John concerning the trinity and unity of the whole godhead, which in his kingdom we shall see face to face, but now, until the Lord comes, we must behold in a glass darkly. It was not only John who drank: the Lord himself has spread John's gospel throughout the world, so that according to each one's capacity all people may drink it.

Each incarnation of the Spirit is creative adoption and adaptation of shapes and forms of the places and times in which we live. When the Spirit and the bride say come, they say it in a language quite other than the commands of presiding officers. Theirs is a world of freedom, of growth and of love; its govern-

---

Oxford. In 1982 he was consecrated titular Bishop of Diokleia and appointed assistant bishop in the Orthodox Archdiocese of Thyateira and Great Britain (under the Ecumenical Patriarchate).

The dialogue was intended as part of a series to be broadcast on Radio Éireann in 1984. In the end this particular programme was never released. I have recorded some of the interview in my book *I Must Be Talking To Myself: Dialogue in the Roman Catholic Church*, Dublin, Veritas, 2004.

21. Augustine on St John's Gospel, Homily 124, 5, 7

ment and structures derive from its inner identity of well-being and self-esteem. Not a council imposing the blueprint of what has already been worked out, but welcoming the sketches of what we do not yet understand. Artists are the natural forgers of such shapes and forms. St John was the consummate artist of Agape. There is no room here for mindless obedience, fearful subservience; this new life inspires creative co-operation with its concomitant asceticism of purposeful achievement. It prompts us to go further because we feel and we embody the tangible reality which such effort has produced in us thus far. The litmus test is life which is difficult to mistake for anything less. The inner glow of energy which has landed, made its home, and penetrated to the quick, is difficult to simulate, impossible to mistake.

The essential mystery of the church is magisterially suzerain, untameably free. This mystery was best understood by the beloved disciple who then, under the guidance of the Holy Spirit, found the words most appropriate to expressing it in language available to our understanding. However, even he recognised that his words were poor and trembling substitutes and that his efforts recorded only a fraction of the reality he sought to convey. 'This is the disciple who testifies to these things and who wrote them down. We know that his testimony is true. Jesus did many other things as well. If every one of them were written down, I suppose that even the whole world would not have room for the books that would be written.'

The theory of the development of doctrine allows us to regard history and the accretions which history involves, as extensions of the principle of incarnation and potential vehicles for the ever guiding Holy Spirit. We should use where possible the infrastructure already laid down over hundreds of years and embrace a movement of evolution rather than of revolution, continuity rather than disruption, as our praxis. The essential ingredient in this integration of the two aspects of the church, its temporal and its spiritual, is humility. Humility is the essential Christian ontology, which effects in us the self-emptying required to allow the Holy Spirit to pervade our being and the being of the church.

The church as an organ of salvation springs from the relationship between Christ and his people. Her role is to lead all people to Christ. The process by which she does this is one of attraction and expulsion. She is a midwife whose role is to give birth to children of God. Once we are in God, her role is to disappear. The church as an historical structure must eventually disappear altogether. When the kingdom comes there will be no further need for earthly paraphernalia. The only thing that endures is love. Love began the church and love is her only end. Her role is to deliver her children over to Christ and then disappear. So the goal of the church is the source of the church: that place, or rather that moment, where she was born and where she must die, each time she gives birth to a new Christian. This is also to distinguish between the church being born and the established church. The source of the church, her birthplace, is outside her juridical and historical structure. Her role is to find this place, this life-giving and death-dealing source, in the person of each one of her members. The church has no place other than in Christ. Her place in the world is simply a way towards that source of her identity. Christ did not come to find a place for God in the world, but rather to show that the world has its place in God. So the church as dinosaur, or the Petrine church, is a necessary though cumbersome outer shell for the church as Spirit, or the Johannine church, which is its inner mystical life of relationship with God.

And this inner mystical relationship is continued throughout history between person and person. Even at the most turbulent and scandalous moments in church history, there was always at least one person who kept the flame of 'right relationship' or orthodoxy alive. Maximus the Confessor (born in 580; died in exile 13 August 662) was one who confessed true belief in who Jesus Christ really was even when Pope Honorius (625 to 638) was ready to condone the monothelite heresy.[22]

---

22. Monothelitism is a teaching which began in Armenia and Syria in AD 633 and held considerable support during the 7th century AD before being officially condemned at the Third Council of Constantinople. It was really an extension of the monophysite position of earlier christological arguments, hammered out in the seven councils previously mentioned. It wanted to believe that Jesus Christ had no human will of his own but had only one divine will. Maximus and others held to the

Later, from the second half of the thirteenth century to the beginning of the fourteenth century, when the church was awash with antipopes, two of the greatest mystics of the world, Julian of Norwich and Catherine of Sienna, kept open the vital connection with the three persons of the Blessed Trinity. In other words, they maintained the vital connection with the three Persons of the Trinity while the church as dinosaur was being led astray.[23]

It is the actual actualisation of the act of incarnation, the re-birth of the Son of God in each member of the Christian community that gives meaning to the forms and contents of the church. It is not the trundling dinosaur of worldly accretions which have attached themselves to the institution like carbuncles to a ship as it crawls through history. The longest dinosaur was apparently Seismosaurus, which measured over 40 metres, as long as five double-decker buses. The external church might well qualify for such a label.

God remains close to the forms of the church if we do not remove them from him. These forms and structures live if the relation, the life with God, is maintained and kept alive within them. This life-giving process is a re-enactment, by the person, of that original primordial life-giving relation. It is that same relation made new in the life of prayer. Prayer places us at that original point: the point of incarnation, of pure, immediate, universal relation which is the arising, the birth, the origin, of word and form. This act of meeting is without continuity and without

---

true doctrine, at great physical cost to himself, that Jesus Christ has two wills (human and divine) corresponding to his two natures.

23. Pope John XXII (1316-34) was opposed by Nicholas V, antipope (1328-1330). Pope Urban VI (1378-89) was opposed by Clement VII, antipope (1378-1394). Pope Boniface IX (1389-1404) was also opposed by Clement VII, antipope (1378-1394), by Benedict XIII, antipope (1394-1417) and John XXIII, antipope (1400-1415); as was Innocent VII (1404-06) by the last two mentioned antipopes. Pope Gregory XII (1406-15) was opposed by no less than three antipopes: Benedict XIII, antipope (1394-1417), John XXIII, antipope (1400-1415) and Alexander V (1409-1410). One might have presumed that the Holy Spirit would have regarded this as three popes too many, but as it turned out it was four too many and the whole lot of them were discarded and Martin V was elected as the 207th successor to St Peter in 1417.

content and therefore a-temporal and infinite. It is the act that once gave birth to the church and the same act that gives birth to her at each moment. Without this unceasing contact with the source of life-giving relation, the form of God in the world becomes dead. God is dead in the world when the act of his incarnation is not kept alive by this dialogue that allows the possibility of dialogue with him. God's eternal presence is at all times and in all places. His presence is like a secret spiritual force that breathes eternally and seeks entry to the world. God cannot enter the world visibly without us. His presence is eternal readiness to give himself to the world. History is an approach to such presence. The various ages of history show a qualitative difference. The earth waits and trembles at the presence of God. At such moments the finger of God touches the silent watcher and the presence becomes revelation, visitation – the earth is allowed to give birth to the form of God. History continues. Certain moments of it are moments of religious genius, the genius of the earth (*humus*) to give birth to God's presence; the genius of humility, that ontological attitude, which allows the act of love to repeat itself in the hearts of people at different times and in different ways in different places.

The fourth and fifth centuries were such times when the mystery of the church was re-enacted so that it produced forms of God in the world which have helped to preserve his presence and keep alive the living memory of his incarnation. All revelations of the one true God are alike in being, they are nothing other than the eternal revelation made perfectly manifest in Jesus Christ. The religious happening is the eternal repetition of the same act of love which gave birth to the church, it is contemporary to the universal and unique act of Jesus Christ who breathed life into it.

PART FOUR

God as Dinosaur

Father, Son and Holy Ghost
by Audre Lorde[1]

I have not ever seen my father's grave.

Not that his judgment eyes have been
forgotten
nor his great hands' print
on our evening doorknobs
    one half turn each night
    and he would come
    drabbled with the world's business
    massive and silent as the whole day's wish
    ready to redefine each of our shapes –
but that now the evening doorknobs wait
and do not recognize us as we pass.

Each week a different woman –
regular as his one quick glass each evening –
pulls up the grass his stillness grows
calling it weed. Each week
A different woman has my mother's face
and he, who time has,
changeless,
must be amazed
who knew and loved but one.
My father died in silence, loving creation
and well-defined response.
He lived
still judgments on familiar things

---

1. Audre Lorde, 'Father, Son and Holy Ghost' from *Collected Poems of Audre Lorde*.

and died
knowing a January 15th that year me.

Lest I go into dust
I have not ever seen my father's grave.

From the beginning we have tried to make a monster out of
our God. I presume it must be some mixture of our *Deus ex
Machina* archetype,[2] our personal experience of oppressive fa-
therhood, or our inferiority complex, which persuades us that
the God who made us is a neurotic tyrant who has been so of-
fended by our radical disobedience that nothing can satisfy his
outraged self-esteem than the blood sacrifice of his only son.
This, we think to ourselves, is the only way God's anger can be
appeased and the sins of the world expiated. The sadistic father
requires the death-dealing punishment of his son, since no one
else is important enough to act as proxy, to appease his terrible
anger at our refusal to obey his commands. This is one of
Christianity's major defamations; but there are others even
more derogatory in the history of world religions.

Nothing could be further from the truth. God has tried, from
the very first revelations of his divine love, to persuade us that
he is lovable, vulnerable, compassionate, and that he has this
unbelievable obsession with us, which will never give up on the
hope that we may love him back. Our problem is a complete
misconception of God, from wherever we inherit it. We are unable for whatever reason to see God as a God of love, forgive-
ness, tenderness and compassion. This seems to stem from our
own inability to believe and to trust that we are loved and valued
in and as we are ourselves.

John Macquarrie[3] talks about the 'humility of God,' pointing
out that the passion and death of Jesus Christ contradicts all our

2. The Latin phrase *deus ex machina* comes from Horace's *Ars Poetica*
where he instructs poets never to resort to a god from the machine to
solve their plots. He refers to the conventions of Greek tragedy, where
a crane was used to lower actors playing gods onto the stage. So a more
generally accurate translation would be 'god from our hands' or 'god
that we make', implying that the god is entirely artificial or conceived
by us.
3. *The Humility of God*, SCM Press Ltd, London, 1978, pp 59-60

conventional ideas about God. This revelation of God is the con-
tradiction of everything that has been commonly believed about
God. 'Almighty God' is our usual way of addressing him, and
'even Christians have tended to think of God as a celestial
monarch, disposing of the world according to his sovereign will,
untouched and untroubled by the storms that rage below.' The
God revealed in Jesus Christ is nothing like the monster in the
sky which we have insisted on trying to venerate; he is a God
who comes 'among us in weakness and humility to stand with
us in the midst of the created order.'

> Where we go wrong is that we bring along some ready-made
> idea of God, wherever we may have learned it, and then we
> try to make Jesus Christ fit in with that idea of God. If we
> take the idea of a revelation of God in Christ seriously, then
> we must be willing to have our understanding of God cor-
> rected and even revolutionised by what we learn in Jesus
> Christ. In other words, we cannot fit Christ into some previ-
> ously established theistic understanding of the world. We
> have to move in the opposite direction, and this means that it
> is through Christ that we have to understand God and his
> relation to the world, so far as we can understand those mat-
> ters. We have to begin with the cross, with what happened
> here on earth and in the course of human history, not with
> the exalted deity on the sapphire throne of pious imagining.
> All our popular ideas of God as the power behind the scene
> who will ensure that everything will turn out well, are shat-
> tered by the Christian understanding of God as the one who
> stands with us in suffering, the eternal Word incarnate in
> Jesus Christ.[4]

The strange relationship which God has developed with us
has not been fashionable among the God-watchers. Angels and
archangels seem to have deplored the amorous connection between God and his chosen ones among the people of Israel. The
Book of Job describes one attempt on their part to discredit this
unworthy object of God's love and God's trembling trust in Job
to be faithful to his love in face of all adversity. However, even

---

4. *The Humility of God*, SCM Press Ltd, London, 1978, pp 63- 67

the chosen people joined the disapproving fray at the sugges-
tion that God would actually become a human being to show his
love and win us over. As well as being folly to the Greeks this
was also scandal to the Jews. But, in the end, it was proof, as St
Paul says, of the height and the depth, the length and the
breadth of God's love for us as human beings.

Since the dawn of human consciousness we have been pro-
jecting our fantasies onto the screen we call God. Abraham Heschel
(1907-1972), a leading Jewish philosopher and Rabbi, has described the Bible as an anthropology for God before it is a theology for us. It shows God just how devious, complicated and
mistrustful we are. The Bible tells the story of our projections
and God's attempts to purify these throughout the history of the
relationship between himself and ourselves. We have distorted,
even vilified this love.

In the end it is not our love for God but God's love for us
which is the initiating and formative part of our mutual relationship. It must be clear to us by now that he is not an all-powerful
dictator, not an omniscient ogre, not a sadistic tyrant. The pre-
personal concepts of God, inherited mostly from Greek philosophy, are bankrupt in the light of God's own revelation of himself. The love of the Trinity, depending as it does on our free ac-
ceptance at each moment, has had to be the most ingenious salvage operation ever imagined. When talking about it, and about
God, we have to use words. There is no gender in God, who is as
much mother as father. I use the masculine pronoun to describe
the person of God only because it has been used traditionally
and overwhelmingly in the Judeo-Christian tradition to which I
belong. There can be no doubt that God as God is neither male
nor female.

At each stubborn refusal to co-operate, at each fearful reject-
ion of what is on offer, at every wilful decision to throw away
the lifeline, the three persons in pursuit have had to regroup and
rearrange their strategy. The hound of heaven comes after us,
hungering for us, needing us. Half the story of our relationship
is his relentless refusal to allow us to give up on him. He has
tried every way possible to show us this love. Eventually he sent
his only beloved Son to become a human being like us. Jesus is
the human face of God. 'Whoever has seen me has seen the

Father.' Jesus shows us who God is through his personality and through his every action from birth to death. These include his childhood, his adolescence, his adulthood. This living seminar on what love means encompasses every social situation, every tiny communication, every human relationship which he underwent. He is the living embodiment of God.

Our culture has been built on a lie and Christianity has helped to promote and sustain that lie. And the lie is this: that it is possible to work out in our heads a logical system which will give us access to ultimate truth. The name of such a system is philosophy and the particular branch of that 'science' which deals with 'being' and places it within our intellectual grasp is 'metaphysics'. Christianity borrowed that system, refined it and inserted into it the geometry of the God who had been revealed in Jesus Christ. The intellectually gifted could understand this intricate system and become masters of metaphysics. They could then teach gifted disciples. The rest would acknowledge that the mystery was too deep for them and would be thankful that there were masters who actually did understand the meaning of such intricacies.

Metaphysics, if it does exist as access to being, is less like mathematics and more like music; that is what the artists of the world have been telling us throughout the centuries. Being is not business. Reality is something we touch rather than grasp.

According to the doctrine of the Trinity, worked out through centuries of attempted communication and self-expression, God lives as a mystery of eternal exchange of love between persons. Their lifestyle is a mutual giving and receiving, a dance of reciprocity. We are invited to share this personal love, which unites us with these three divine persons. Essentially our being is also mystery. It comes from the Father of all that is, who is unknown, unknowable and never to be fully understood. Before this silent and unutterable mystery, every human being is by definition agnostic.

As Christians we have been given a glimpse of the Trinitarian God through the incarnation of the Son. Jesus Christ is the human face of the Trinity. He is therefore knowable, as one of us. The danger is that we take this gift and turn it into a magic formula. We then become Gnostics, those who claim to know; those with the secret knowledge of God unavailable to others outside our group. Whereas our Christianity should mean that we are neither gnostics nor agnostics but rather diagnostics who can prescribe the way forward between the known and the unknown through the ongoing dialogue with each other in the Holy Spirit. Whereas Christ, the second Person of the Trinity, became incarnate in our human nature, the Holy Spirit, as Third Person of the Trinity, impregnates our person. This is the mystery of Pentecost, the deepest and most intimate revelation about who God is and who we really are.

* * *

The word *perichoresis* was used to describe the ambience of God as we have been allowed to glimpse this reality through various kinds of revelation. It is within such a loving space that the three divine persons infiltrate one another reciprocally, without invasion. We are offered access to this delicate household. The ultimate theological error or heresy is thinking of God as living in an altogether different sphere from us without any possible contact. Since the incarnation of God the Son, we share the same household. We are children of this household. Although we cannot be divine by nature, we have become so by adoption. This is a problem for us, as it is for many adopted children: to really believe that we are part of the household. However, it is *our* problem. God has gone to infinite pains to assure us of this fact. And such involvement has also made a difference to the Trinity of persons, who in some strange way are more fully themselves by this multiple outlet for their self-giving identity.

Perichoresis is a Greek term used to describe the triune relationship between the three persons in the one Godhead. The idea is rooted in those statements of the New Testament where the relationship of Father, Son, and Holy Spirit is said to be 'in' each other, while they themselves remain distinct as persons. An incorrect etymology of the Greek term suggested that *peri* meaning around, and *choresis* meaning to dance (from the same root as 'choreography'), offered an image of the relationship between the Persons of the Trinity as an eternal holy dance of each Person around and within the Others. However, this etymology has been questioned by the experts of Greek philology as an interpretive move rather than an etymological accuracy. The full concept which was to be given technical expression in the term *perichoresis*, especially as translated into Latin in *circumincessio* by Hilary of Arles, derives from the verb *chorein* meaning both 'to go,' 'to make room for' or 'to contain'.

To me, these quibbles about etymology do not change much the direction in which we are being prompted to go. This word is describing how three persons can be together in a mutual love which never allows one to dominate or disparage the others. This can be a 'dance,' or a 'containment,' or a 'making room for,' as long as the perfect freedom, identity and unity are maintained. Mutual interpenetration is one way of putting it. Alister McGrath explains that the term 'allows the individuality of the persons to be maintained, while insisting that each person shares in the life of the other two. An image often used to express this idea is that of a "community of being", in which each person, while maintaining its distinctive identity, penetrates the others and is penetrated by them.'[5]

The first recorded usage of the term in this context is in the writings of John Damascene (676-749) who described it as a 'cleaving together'. The Father, the Son and the Holy Spirit not only embrace each other, but they also enter into each other, permeate each other, and dwell in each other. One in being, they are also always one in the intimacy of their friendship. Perichoresis is a fellowship of three co-equal beings perfectly embraced in love and harmony, expressing an intimacy that no one can humanly comprehend. This is what we need to develop, not only between each other, but also between all three parts of our triune brain, so that every part of us can be hoisted in a spiral towards the infinite and eternal communion which is our privileged calling as divinely loved human beings.

---

5. Alister McGrath, *Christian Theology: An Introduction*, 3rd ed, Blackwell, 2001

PART FIVE

Dancing with Dinosaurs

You are at the moment directly approaching the divine;
more, you are flying straight towards it,
irresistibly surmounting all obstacles.

But I have been there, always,
even as a child,
and I am returning thence on foot.

I have been sent back,
not to proclaim it,
but to be among what is human,
to see everything and reject nothing,
not one of those thousand transformations
in which the absolute disguises itself,
vilifies itself,
and makes itself unrecognisable.

I am like a man gathering fungi and healing herbs among the
weeds,
who appears to be bent and occupied with small things
whilst the tree trunks around him stand and pray.

But a time will come when I shall prepare the potion.
And yet another when I shall mount upwards with it,
this potion, in which everything is distilled and combined,
the most poisonous and deadly elements as well,
because of their strength.

And I will take it up to God,
so that he may slake his thirst,
and feel his own glory running through his veins.[1]

---

1. Letter written by Rainer Maria Rilke to Clara Rilke from 77 Rue de Varenne, Paris, 4 September, 1908, *Briefe* 1907-1914, p 48

The spirituality which involves the deification of our whole humanity must acknowledge the serpent in us and assume the sum total of who we are into heaven. Dancing with the dinosaurs means, in this perspective, an attempt to rehabilitate that essential part of ourselves which is the serpent within. Far from being evil, this serpentine brain is part of the very essence of who we are as human beings. Rehabilitation of the serpent within needs the arbitration of the limbic brain, the seat of poetic utterance, between the abstract scientist and the older stalwart underneath. There can be no question of the domination of one part of the brain over the others. This has been the mistake of many forms of asceticism which sought to impose an abstract ideal upon the more primitive brain even to the point of annihilation. Such would be the kind of spirituality which Rilke calls 'directly approaching the divine; more, flying straight towards it, irresistibly surmounting all obstacles.' Rather than domination of one part of the brain over the other two, there should be dialogue between all three which valorises the particularity of each. For whatever reason, in the past, we have tended to equate 'spirituality' with the eradication of our serpentine selves. Not only has this led to imbalance but it is the source of many difficulties which have only recently come visibly and publicly to the fore. The serpent raising its ugly head, as commentators might describe recent scandals of various kinds, might also be understood as the inevitable consequences of neglecting the ineradicable dinosaur within ourselves.

Whatever way you look at it, the Roman Catholic Church has declared *ex cathedra* and dogmatically, otherwise nobody would ever imagine or believe it, that there was a man and there was a woman living on this planet who were so intimately connected with two of the persons of the Holy Trinity that they are now both fully alive and well and living with God the Father forever. The man is hardly a problem because he was God, the Son, the Second Person of the Trinity incarnate, who came on earth and lived for thirty-three years in Palestine until he was put to death by crucifixion.

The Son of God became one of us so that we might be deified is the full reality of what we believe. In the pithy phrase of St Athanasius: 'He became human so that we might become divine.'

What does it mean to become divine and how does it happen? These are the questions which need to be answered and, although Christianity clings to the statements or the dogmas, there is much disagreement about the way in which such things happen and the way in which we explain them to ourselves.

Jesus Christ, the second person of the Trinity, became a man by his one person assuming our human nature. His assumption of our nature made our nature divine by adoption. Our nature and God's nature are absolutely different and there has never been a question of our nature becoming God's nature or vice versa. The mystery happens through the agency of the person. 'In his own person he killed the hostility' as the letter to the Ephesians puts it.[2] Christ's person is the second person of the Trinity who became man. His person as man is that same person. It is the Holy Spirit who descends on our person in baptism and makes us participators in the divine life of the Trinity. This divine life is all about love and it enlarges our hearts until they become eternal and infinite and we become deified. So, the person is the instrument of this happening. Some suggest that we are given a new person with our baptism, an ecclesial personhood.[3] I do not believe this. Grace builds on nature, and whatever the person is, which makes us who we are, from the beginning of our own personhood, this has to be the same person which becomes divine by the working of the Holy Spirit.

We begin our lives as limited temporal persons but we attain to infinity and eternity because our persons are transformable and expandable to these dimensions. The 'who we are' as persons from the beginning of our lives is expandable and adaptable to eternity and infinity. What do we mean when we say that as human persons, as creatures of God, we become *capax infiniti* or *capax aeterni*, capable of eternity and infinity? We do not mean, we cannot mean, that we become capable of either containing or becoming God. Only the three divine persons of the Trinity contain one another and exist as God in the absolute

---

2. Ephesians, ch 2 v 16b in the New Jerusalem Bible translation.
3. John D. Zizioulas, *Being as Communion*, St Vladimir's Seminary Press, New York, 1993; and *Communion and Otherness*, Continuum, New York, 2006. I have learnt so much from this author that it seems petty to be quoting his two books because of one tiny point of disagreement.

freedom which this requires. We, on the other hand, as dance partners of these same persons of the Trinity, become capable of experiencing 'conjointly what cannot be experienced separately, that is union and communion with God,' and sharing the inexhaustible benefits of such relationship.[4] We only have to aim ourselves in those directions and adapt ourselves accordingly. And here we must recognise that the principle of Incarnation requires that every iota of our human personality is eventually assumed into heaven and becomes the divine person we were destined to be. This means, practically speaking, that the human brain which arrives on earth in an unfinished condition is able to build for itself, and add to itself, all that is necessary for eternal life. We are potentially gods when we arrive, but we have to work at it to allow our humanity to break through to these possibilities. Like every other worthwhile task we accomplish on earth, this requires effort, diligence and practice. Such is the meaning of the ascetical life: that we train and trim for eternal life.

What 'person' actually is, remains a mystery, whether in terms of God or of ourselves. However, it is not something entirely beyond our grasp, because it is a reality which we live every moment of our lives, as well as being the reality which underpins everything that we are. Although we may not be able to scoop it up from the foundations of our being to examine it clinically in the mirror of our minds, it is still a basic reality with which we are in profound and continuous contact. So, it is through this mystery that we connect and are able to become part of the communion which is the three persons of the Trinity for ever and ever. To become that and to enjoy it for all eternity requires effort on our part, although the effort is mostly giving way and sinking back into the supernatural splendour which is the mystery of the three persons of the Trinity in communion with one another and sempiternally dwelling in our hearts.

4. Human personhood must be understood as human. The eschatological fulfilment of the person (who cannot be abstracted from his or her nature) does not entail elimination of all creaturely limitation or all creaturely necessity, which would mean the elimination of the creaturely as such. *The Theology of John Zizioulas, Personhood and the Church*, edited by Douglas H. Night, Ashgate, Hampshire, 2007, ch 5 'Persons and Particularity' by Colin Gunton, pp 97-124

God becoming man in Jesus Christ is a tantalising seducer who leaves us worse off than before he came, unless the Third Person of the Trinity intervenes to shift the focus of attraction and bring us back to earth within ourselves. The Holy Spirit is God indwelling in our particular personhood. We become the mystical body of Christ because of his assumption of our nature, his body and blood reality as one of us. But each one of us is what Jesus Christ was, and each one of us is now where Jesus Christ is for all eternity, through the ingenuity of the Holy Spirit. This is the meaning of the mystery of the Ascension: Jesus leaving the disciples so that we find God in ourselves. They had no sense of the new kind of personhood we are invited to become. They were grieving for him, looking up into the sky, until an angel was sent to tell them to focus on the earth, to focus on ourselves.

Jesus Christ's humanity, his mission, his blessing, can only be accomplished by his leaving us in body and returning to us in the Person of the Holy Spirit who merges into the flame and the quick of each individual person's personal life. This internal Christ consciousness is induced in us by Christ's having moved outwards and upwards himself. The disciples cannot receive this Holy Spirit until Christ goes and leaves them. The Holy Spirit is God indwelling in each one of us personally, and not God incarnate in Christ.

The difficulty for us as Christians is that, like the first disciples, we have allowed ourselves to get fixated with the earthly life and especially the gruesome death of Jesus Christ while he was here on earth. We somehow seem to have persuaded ourselves that his deification required crucifixion as its prerequisite, and that any of us who wish to follow in his footsteps need to be crucified also.

Divine love moves us upwards, makes us stand up and rise from the dead. Because the vertical line of resurrection is crossed by the horizontal line of heredity, the way we are by our human birth conflicts with the way we should be by resurrection. Such is the tree of the cross of human existence, such is the sign of the cross as source of our blessing.

The cross of Christ is the tree of life. The tree as growth upwards and outwards is the model for any such spiral growth.

Trees, like the rest of us, if they had their natural way, would crawl and spread like roots along the ground. It is only because they need sun that they force themselves upwards and reach for the light. This means that they grow both horizontally and verti- cally, making progress upwards and outwards inch by inch every year. Rainer Maria Rilke says:

> I cannot conceive that the cross should remain, which was, after all, only a cross-roads. It certainly should not be stamped on us on all occasions like a brand-mark. For he in- tended simply to provide the loftier tree, on which we could ripen better. He, on the cross, is this new tree in God, and we were to be warm, happy fruit, at the top of it. This tree should have become so one with us, or we with it, and by it, that we should not need to occupy ourselves continually with it, but simply and quietly with God, for his aim was to lift us up into God more purely. Do not always force us back into the labour and sorrow that it cost him to 'redeem' us. Let us, at last, enter into this state of redemption.[5]

The 'sign of the cross' was paramount for early Christianity. The Middle Ages and more morose 19th century spirituality emphasised the Man of Sorrows, the Suffering Saviour, and the cross became a crucifix, with sometimes the most gory represent- ations of the dying body of Christ affixed. This aspect of the total mystery overshadowed all the rest and people were encouraged to revel in their own suffering and affliction, of whatever kind, in solidarity and sympathy with the suffering servant.

The projection of our own pathology and fixation upon one particular aspect of the total mystery swaps the glory for the gore, and trades a birthright for a mess of pottage. The crucifix- ion is not a fact. It cannot be nailed down to one explanation, labelled with one easy heading. It is an event. It incorporates the whole drama of God's love for us and of our new existence in him. To concentrate upon the cross as an instrument of torture and death is to wrap ourselves in the cocoon, when we should be in flight with the butterfly.

The sign of the cross should be the quintessence of the spirit-

5. Rainer Maria Rilke, *Rodin and Other Prose Pieces*, Quartet Books, London, 1986, pp 144-146

ual quest. The four spatial directions of the compass join together with the depth of the centre. Just as we have five senses and five fingers with which to probe the world around us, so this pentagram will be significant in probing the world of the spirit. Under this sign, blessing or benediction flows. Each of the wounds of Christ are effective against the five dark currents of human motivation: the desire to be great, the desire to take, the desire to keep, the desire to advance at the expense of others, the desire to hold on to, at the expense of others. The five wounds of Christ were a five sense breakthrough into our world of the greedy senses and covetous limbs. His wounds are five boreholes which allow the five currents of the human will to be impregnated from above by the will of God. This is the 'sign of the cross,' the pentagram of the five wounds.

A wound is a door. The eye, for instance, is a wound covered by a mobile skin which we call an eyelid. Our eyes are open wounds. So are our other senses. They are wounds through which the world imposes itself on us. The five senses are organs of perception, not of action. They are passive receptors. The five organs of action, on the other hand, are our two legs, our two arms, and our head. These must develop analogous wounds which will become the stigmata of our alignment to the cross of the divine will. The head, however, does not bear the fifth wound, as we know from the paradigm of the Christian mystery. It bears the crown of thorns. These are the openings which allow for interdigitation between all three parts of our brain and with the promptings of the Holy Spirit.

The fifth wound is the wound of the heart, the wound of organic humility which replaces the natural current of the human will. The twentieth century made us more than ever aware of the currents of natural energy which normally motivate us and spur us to action. Three philosophers suggested one such instinct as the primary motivation for everything we do or say. Freud nominated sex, Nietzsche the will-to-power, and Marx thought money made the world go round.

In a corresponding assignation from the other side of the spectrum, generations of spiritual seekers stemmed the flow of these natural currents of selfishness by taking three corresponding vows: the vow of poverty attacks greed; the vow of chastity wounded lust; the vow of obedience attacks the will-to-power.

The only wound through which grace can flow is the freely opened human heart and will of an authentic lover of God. The bridge between them is created through open wounds on both sides. The pentagram of the five wounds is the victory sign of the Divine breakthrough. The freedom it has won for us is so powerful that it can lead us through every one of our five senses to a hell of our own construction. That is what freedom means: the free choice of surrender to heaven or construction of hell from our own sweating selves. The secret wisdom hidden from the beginning of time is the mystery of God's love for us. And so powerful is this secret wisdom that the five gates of hell shall never prevail against the formula of the five wounds. This is what is meant by 'infallibility' – that the Holy Spirit will never allow the dinosaur of the church to lead it astray. But we must learn to dance with the dinosaur.

Life with and in the Holy Spirit makes us persons in the fullest sense of the word, which is that Word spoken by the Second Person of the Trinity. And the Word was God. We become a new creation, a combination of humanity and divinity which is the ultimate in creativity on both sides of the border between God and us. We allow divinity to penetrate our being in 'bright shoots of everlastingness' as another poet describes the effect.

The Holy Spirit makes us members of a new species, 'living from the religious centre of personal energy where spiritual emotions are the habitual core'. Such was the scientific observation of William James over a hundred years ago in his attempt to describe the *Varieties of Religious Experience*.[6] The new creation, the new kind of humanity, develops its own particular intensity of passion, its own kind of emotional life. When a certain intensity is attained by the new emotion 'the new ardor which burns in his breast consumes in its glow the lower "uses" which formerly beset him, and keeps him immune against infection from the entire groveling portion of his nature.' This is what James calls 'the expulsive power of a higher affection.'[7] It is the way in

6. William James, *Varieties of Religious Experience*, London: 1904, p 212
7. Ibid, p 208

which the person deals with the triune brain and incorporates the serpentine and the limbic into a different register. The natural mechanism of our possessive and addictive tendencies is harnessed to a higher motivation. It can be described as a 'conversion,' a change of currency, a removal of one fuse and its replacement by another. 'To get to it, a critical point must usually be passed, a corner turned within one. Something must give way, a native hardness must break down and liquefy.'[8]

If Christ is the image of the Father, the Holy Spirit is the image of the Son. For although equal in every way, the mission of the Holy Spirit is to show to believers throughout time the character of the incarnated one, and thus allow us to see, through him, the Father. The Son makes known the Father, and the Holy Spirit bears witness to the Son.

The mystery of the Holy Spirit is so intimate and subtle that it can easily be misrepresented. The Second Person of the Trinity became incarnate in the human body of a particular historical identity, Jesus of Nazareth. The Holy Spirit becomes implanted in the person of each and every one of us and sows the seed so that we become, in our turn, mother of God. We give birth to God in ourselves. All the mysteries which Christianity has celebrated so specifically in terms of Mary the Mother of God are applicable to each of us. Through the Spirit, with the Spirit, in the Spirit, the mystical body of the communion of saints is personified allowing Christ to play 'in ten thousand places,/lovely in limbs, and lovely in eyes not his/To the father through the features of men's faces' (Hopkins).

The three Persons of the Trinity have all been involved from the outset of creation in the specific roles which each assumes in the economy of salvation. The Holy Spirit has always been at work everywhere in the world. Everywhere, that is, where persons of good will were ready and willing to unite their unique personhood with the Divine Personhood of this Third Person of the Trinity. Incarnation of the Son happens through assumption of flesh-and-blood humanity; impregnation by the Spirit happens wherever a human person allows entry to their person by the self-effacing Spirit. Christians have been so mesmerised by

8. Ibid, p 99

the invasive surgery achieved so dramatically by the Second Person of the Trinity that we have sometimes lost sight of the more long-term and widespread homoeopathy which has been from the beginning, and will be to the end of time, the prerogative of the Third Person of the Trinity. The two arms of the Father have been truncated and foreshortened to the human hands of the Son. There is much more to the divine plan for salvation of the world than a thirty-three-year life history of one Jewish man, even though he is God in human form. The Holy Spirit was at work before, during and after that plenipotentiary moment of Divine Self-Revelation. The Divine plan involves all three Persons working together in really distinct idioms, while, at the same time, in complete harmony and complementarity. The inspiration of the Spirit leads those who truly seek God towards the still point of the turning world situated 'in' Christ. But not a Christ triumphantly arrayed in the garments and the customs of one particular culture. Rather a naked Christ stripped of every vestige of ethnic identity; a zero Christ who has emptied himself to the point of death where he can become completely one with our common humanity; a post-Christian Christ, leaving us himself as the greatest blessing ever bestowed on our humanity, nothingness in Person. Leaving us to find out who we really are. 'Christ is nothing' Kierkegaard whispers, 'never forget it, Christianity.' The cross of Christ is a vortex fed by radiating quadrants from the four corners of the world. The word 'universe' means turned into one. There are prophetic priests working all over the planet who are burrowing their way towards this one vertical escape route.

Everything about the life of Jesus Christ is encompassed in a web woven by the Holy Spirit. His birth, his baptism, his hour of triumph, were the Holy Spirit impregnating the womb, breathing on the waters, lifting him up. At his death Jesus 'crying out in a loud voice, yielded up his spirit'[9] or, in another account of the same event, breathed his last having cried out in a loud voice 'Father, into your hands I commend my spirit'[10] quoting from Ps 30:6. These scriptures, also written under the inspiration of the

---

9. Matthew 27:50
10. Luke 23:46

Holy Spirit, are recognising that at this axial moment in the history of the Holy Trinity's rescue operation of the world, the man Jesus had emptied himself so completely that there was nothing left in him to prevent complete inspiration of the Holy Spirit. The person of Christ is the linchpin from which all else hangs. We can all use his person to attach ourselves to the mystery of salvation, the mystery of our communion with the three persons of the Trinity and with each other forever. At moments of such perfect obedience and alignment of wills as Christ experienced on the cross, every other human person can become fully one with the Holy Spirit of God and can call it 'my' spirit.

In certain vocabularies about the inner workings of the Blessed Trinity, about which others prefer to remain silent, it is the Son who is 'generated' and therefore, in our human order, it is the Son who is born; but following this selfsame economy of Trinitarian personhood, the Spirit 'proceeds' from the Father and this is an endless and ubiquitous procession which can inspire any particular person or persons willing to co-operate with the energy of this invisible and lifegiving Spirit. Christ was born, Christ has died, Christ has left the planet in Person. The Spirit was never born, never died and will never leave the planet until every single person has been shepherded into the one, holy, catholic and apostolic plan of salvation which all three persons of the Trinity have been trying to implement, while at all times respecting the infuriatingly unpredictable free will of each and every one of us. This was, and is, the unimaginably generous game plan from the outset.

This is an attitude we adopt, indeed a person we become, if we are to plumb the secret depths and decode the hidden knowledge of God. It requires a kind of attention or awareness essential for spiritual activity of any kind. There is a particular kind of concentration applicable to play or to dance which can allow you be a tight-rope walker. If you concentrate on each step you take you will fall. We must foster the intelligence of the rhythmic system, the participation of both the respiratory and circulatory systems which replace the working of the third level of the brain during such acrobatic feats. Theologically speaking, in the Christian tradition, this is the mystery of *kenosis*, the Greek word for self-emptying. In the case of the Man-God, Jesus

Christ there was a double *kenosis*. He emptied himself of his Godhead so that he could become a person in our world. His life on earth was a further self-emptying of that nature (ours) which he had assumed, right to the point zero, the draining of the last drop on the cross where the ultimate fusion occurred and the explosion of resurrection into a new kind of being, a new kind of loving occurred.

Dancing for us is a movement and a direction similar to this second kind of *kenosis*. It is also surrender. We empty ourselves until we reach that same point zero of our humanity, the very last skin between us and the abyss of nothingness, beyond which is the absolute otherness of God. When we reach that source of ourselves, that original point, that openness to the void at the very last extreme of what we are, we find there a bridge which has been erected by, with, and through the person of Jesus Christ. He is the *pontifex*, the bridgebuilder. The bridge is one that moves out over the abyss from two opposite sides and joins in the middle without actually merging or being soldered into one. It meets but leaves a tantalisingly unnoticeable gap between each of the two sections. It is possible to meet on the bridge, but the two sides yet remain irretrievably rooted in the banks of their respective foundations and never achieve the merger at the centre which would cause them to dissolve into one another. The bridgeable gap between the two is maintained by the tension which allows both to remain forever always on the point of meeting. It is the place prepared for us since the beginning of time, what St Paul expresses so enigmatically in a pre-position (almost a dis-position) Εν Χριστω (*en Christo*) ('in' Christ) which is that link, that space between; forged through the person of Christ, in his divinity for all time, through his humanity at one specific historical moment, which is the stainless steel, tension-filled, parallel interface, bridging the gap without eliminating it, which allows availability, without full access, from either side of the divide.

There is no necessity for us to be aware of the theological infrastructure put in place by divine engineering, not merely since Jesus Christ came on earth but, as St Paul says, from the beginning of time. This ingenious salvage operation constantly being implemented by the Trinity, has been made available in blueprint to those who have the privilege of initiation to the mysteries of Christianity as a religion. For the rest of humankind, even those who have never heard of Jesus Christ, the delicate infrastructure remains in place. It is possible for anyone to reach the outer limits, the cliffside, starting from whatever geographical or historical point happens to be their station of departure. They can then walk that bridge without either knowing what it is, or how it came to be. In technical theological terms, this is what is meant by saying that the achievement of hypostatic union is an ontological reality for all time.

So, what prevents us from finding and using this bridge? Many many things. Fear, guilt, ignorance, a sense of inferiority, unworthiness, uncleanness, these and other mists and fogs which pervade our being, make it difficult for us to love or be loved. Especially when the lover is all-holy, all-pure, all-powerful.

Freedom is what we need. Freedom from fear; freedom to love. Two things seem to be essential as preliminaries to any kind of relationship with God. The first is best expressed in the words nakedness, openness, vulnerability, whatever allows us to be there in his presence in the stark reality of who we are. The second is whatever allows us to love and accept this reality in its every aspect, and to trust that God also finds it loveable and acceptable to him. Both are probably summed up in a correct understanding of 'humility'.

A friend of mine wrote to me recently describing her natural ability to dance and specifically to dance with one particularly gifted partner: 'I had always loved dancing; but somewhere along the way, in my early 20s, I learned to dance really well – almost overnight; I had no will of my own but gave myself up to my partner. If he had a sense of rhythm I could follow whatever he did and he was a beautiful dancer – the best.' I have not heard a better description of prayer as dancing with the dinosaur.

The essential purpose of this book is to remind ourselves of the depth and complexity of the persons whom we really are. Without acknowledging and incorporating every aspect of this total personality, we are incapable of relating to anyone else. We have been inclined, especially in the more recent past, to valorise the part of our brain which corresponds to the neocortex and to suppress, if not deny, the other two equally important layers of our make-up. Such denial and suppression has been especially true of Roman Catholic Christianity in Ireland. We have been brought up on stories about St Patrick driving out the snakes from Ireland as if the snake represented all that is evil. Evidence suggests that post-glacial Ireland never had snakes, but the myth that St Patrick banished them can be interpreted as meaning that Christianity in its Irish form was a colonisation of the other two parts of the brain, both the emotional and the serpentine by the abstract neo-cortex. Such domination by one part over the other two can only lead to havoc, as indeed it has done.

From the beginning, our species has been fashioned in the 'image of God.' And that image has always been both male and female. The second human being who has been dogmatically declared by the Roman Catholic Church to have entered definitively and eternally into divinity is Mary the Mother of Jesus. She could be described as humility in person. As a woman it was more difficult for our overwhelmingly patriarchal society to provide her with a passport and the requisite qualifications for residency among the three persons of the Trinity. But eventually, after much deliberation she was certified as assumed into heaven, body and soul, and will remain there with the other three persons of the Trinity for all eternity.

Let's forget about how she got there for the moment and concentrate on the fact that it wasn't just part of her; it was the whole reality of her, who she was, as a young girl in Galilee, an unmarried mother, who is now transformed into a divine creature, treasured by the three persons of the eternal Godhead. And this declaration was made in 1950 at a time when patriarchal domination in the world was at its peak and the role of women and their status in society at its nadir. C.G. Jung considered the 1950 dogma of the Assumption of Mary into Heaven as the 'most important spiritual development since the Reformation.' Why? Because it honoured the 'feminine principle' in the Godhead, as he put it. More importantly for us it makes it clear that we as a species, both male and female, have all that is necessary in our make-up to stretch ourselves towards infinity and are capable of realizing our destinies as everlasting and divine persons.

The danger for us is that having made this declaration about one of ourselves in our capacity to become divine we then take it all back by ascribing to Mary a status which removes her completely from her humanity and her direct relationship and consanguinity with us. Such might be the popular interpretation of the Immaculate Conception of Mary which was deemed to be a necessary prelude both to her motherhood of God and to her Assumption into heaven. This also is a dogmatic teaching of the Roman Catholic Church which we must hold, treasure and believe. But we must acknowledge it as a mystery and strive to understand it in all its splendour and subtlety. What it cannot mean is that Mary is removed from any aspect of the full humanity to which we all belong.

The dogma of the Immaculate Conception of Mary – referring to Mary's sinlessness, 'full of grace' and 'blessed among women' (Luke 1:28) – was proclaimed in 1854. How easy it might have been for a particular generation to equate 'conceived without sin' with 'conceived without sex.' All of which might seem to equate the serpent with sin, evil and Satan. In terms of our triune brain, the imagery of twelve stars crowning her head and the crushing of the serpent under her feat, seems to imply that the neo-cortex is eliminating, or trying to eliminate, the serpentine brain in order to become sinless. This is the ambiguity which has dogged most notions of purity throughout the centuries of Christendom.

Although most Christians and Muslims believe that Mary was without sin and 'immaculate' (meaning without stain), they would not agree about the precise meaning of these words. The dogma of the Immaculate Conception is one which would benefit greatly from dialogue throughout the whole church. The Eastern Christian Church first celebrated a feast of the Conception of the Most Holy and All Pure Mother of God on 9 December, perhaps as far back as the fifth century in Syria. By the seventhth century it was a widely known feast in the East. However, the early use of the term *achrantos* or 'spotless' with reference to the Virgin Mary needs clarification. While the Eastern Church called Mary *achrantos* (spotless or immaculate), it did not define exactly what this meant. Today the majority of Orthodox Christians would not accept the scholastic definition of Mary's preservation from original sin before her birth that subsequently evolved into the Catholic doctrine of the Immaculate Conception after the Great Schism of 1054. In the Islamic tradition of Muhammad, Mary and her Son were the only children who could not be touched by Satan at the moment of their birth, for God imposed a veil between them and Satan.

Statistics reveal that any woman born in the year 2011 will be expected to live until she is 120. Several people I have mentioned this to suggested that, if they had known this beforehand they might have looked after themselves a bit better earlier on. Christianity says very much more than this. It holds that we are going to live forever, and that whoever we are now at this moment, has got all that is required, whether actually or potentially, to achieve this goal. In other words, the plasticity of our triune brain is capable of stretching itself to the power of infinity.

The evolution which we must achieve will be a transformation and elevation of the whole human being to a level where the imperatives of biology will not be as pressing or overpowering as they are by nature. Such transformation will be achieved by a kind of loving which is more specifically human, more personal, more total. The medieval theologians had a phrase in Latin, *amor transit in conditionem objecti* which means, more or less, that love transports us into the situation or condition of the loved one. We become like the one we love. And this happens more dramatically when the lover is as totally different from ourselves as God is. But the use of the word love here is what we mean, all of us, by the word love. It is not some unrecognisable substitute which we call 'love' because we are addressing ourselves to God. It is still our wonderfully romantic and exciting notion of being in love, but stretched to infinity, packed with ice, stitched with salt, multiplied incrementally beyond everything we have ever experienced or imagined. It is love everlasting. And to achieve it we have to make the necessary preparations.

Such love happens between us as human beings, as well as between us and God. Love between partners who allow the time, the struggle, the patience and the relentless persistence necessary to reveal to one another the height and the depth, the length and the breadth of their own mysterious personhood, is a similar kind of fruit. Couples who stay together do not become different people but they grow into one another. Octavio Paz calls love the point of intersection between desire and reality. 'Love reveals reality to desire.' Love is the magic middle term 'creating the transition from the erotic object to the beloved person.' Love makes whoever you were originally obsessed by into a reality, if you can wait around long enough to find out, and weather the storms and the shocks which such a heady transformation process of necessity entails. Love is the energy that moves us into God and effects the necessary transformation of our biological way of being in the process.

So that such love does change us from being possessive and grasping individuals to becoming open and radiating centres of generosity. Such openness allows the energy of divine love to stretch us to infinity. This has happened to Mary the Mother of God and if she can do it, we can do it, that is the meaning of the communion of saints. We are created with the built-in possibility of divine relationship leading towards eventual divinisation. But we need to include every aspect of ourselves in this transformation. We need to 'mount upwards with it,/ this potion, in which everything is distilled and combined,/ the most poisonous and deadly elements as well,/ because of their strength.' And these are the elements associated with the serpentine brain, which must not be excluded.

The mystery of Christianity is also that God wanted to become human. And we have to help God in that endeavour. We have to take up to God everything about ourselves in a cup of salvation 'so that he may slake his thirst/ and feel his own glory running through his veins.' C. G. Jung puts it strikingly: 'Ever since John the apocalyptist experienced for the first time (perhaps unconsciously) that conflict into which Christianity inevitable leads, mankind has groaned under this burden: God wanted to become man, and still wants to.'[11] We are the way in which this ultimately happens. 'For Christ plays in ten thousand places,/ Lovely in limbs, and lovely in eyes not his' (Hopkins).

---

11. C. G. Jung, Answer to Job, CW 11 §739